Around-The-World Family

STORIES OF ADVENTURE & GRACE

Around-The-World Family

STORIES OF ADVENTURE & GRACE

John J. Norton

FOREWORD BY ADAM R. LEE

Around-the-World Family: Stories of Adventure & Grace

© 2022 New Reformation Publications

Published by:
1517 Publishing
PO Box 54032
Irvine, CA 92619-4032

Publisher's Cataloging-In-Publication Data
(Prepared by The Donohue Group, Inc.)

Names: Norton, John J., 1971- author. | Lee, Adam R., writer of supplementary textual content.
Title: Around-the-world family : stories of adventure & grace / by John J. Norton ; foreword by Adam R. Lee.
Description: Irvine, CA : 1517 Publishing, [2022]
Identifiers: ISBN 9781948969888 (paperback) | ISBN 9781948969895 (ebook)
Subjects: LCSH: Norton, John J., 1971—Travel—Anecdotes. | Foreign study—Anecdotes.
  | Culture—Study and teaching (Higher)—Anecdotes. | Voluntarism—Anecdotes.
  | LCGFT: Travel writing. | Anecdotes.
Classification: LCC LB2376 .N67 2022 (print) | LCC LB2376 (ebook) | DDC 370.116—dc23

Printed in the United States of America

Cover art by Zachariah James Stuef

TABLE OF CONTENTS

FOREWORD

One of my first and favorite memories of the plans that would eventually become the Around-the-World Semester came at the end of a long meal in the cafeteria at Concordia University, Irvine. I had just finished laying out a rough sketch of a 16-week backpacking trip for 20 students that consisted of both academic courses and short-term mission projects, and then asking John Norton if he and his family could imagine themselves co-leading such an adventure. John dialed his wife Erica from the table, and soon the whole cafeteria shook with the scream that blasted from his phone. It was a shout of joy, followed by Erica's exclamation of something like: "This is exactly what I've been praying about forever!"

Few people back in California were truly aware of the many risks and sacrifices the Norton Family accepted each time they backpacked together around the world. Jack and Naomi were taken out of their excellent Christian schools in Orange County and given self-paced home-school curriculum. As a family they risked unknown health conditions and questionable medical care, unknown cooking conditions and questionable foods, and unknown road conditions and questionable vehicles. They had to leave their close-knit church family and neighborhood community and find house-sitters to care for their home. They had to prepare, pack, and portage enough curricula, clothes, medicine, and even diapers to last months.

Most people we met while traveling, however, were acutely aware and deeply moved by the risks and sacrifices made so that the whole Norton Family could serve alongside them in their ministries and schools. No family is perfect, but in this glass bowl of practicing a 24-hour ministry of presence with our students and mission partners, God blessed the Nortons and their children on these trips with the love, grace, and patience to be as darn close to perfect as I've ever witnessed on the road. The kids themselves were led by the Holy Spirit in so many mission ways. I can still clearly see Jack gathering crowds of local kids to play soccer, Naomi melting the heart of a Turkish imam, and Sheffield's adorableness drawing people of all generations into closer fellowship with our teams.

I enjoyed advantages of time and freedom as a single professor and leader, but God needed a professor with a family as well to be at the core of our leadership team. On each trip, God used the Nortons' transparent examples as husband, wife, and parents not only as inspiring role models for our students, but also as a healing influence for some of our students who came from broken homes. The family structure of the Nortons radiated out to form a family structure of the whole team during our four to five months on the road. This family structure helped us all focus on something outside ourselves and prepared us better for serving alongside others in the many varied mission contexts we experienced.

The stories in this book not only show the wisdom God has taught John through the unique and humble individuals we served alongside during our circumnavigations, but they also spring from the risk-embracing and God-trusting community of his family and the students we traveled with (and of course the prayers of the many families back home). God added these adopted brothers and sisters around the world to our family as He let us all taste and see the gladness of being a part of the borderless family of God.

Adam Lee
Mission Partner in Germany
with the Mission of Christ Network
Former assistant professor at Concordia University Irvine

PREFACE

We bounced in four-wheel-drive vehicles for 27 hours to reach Mamling, a small Nepali village deep in the foothills of the Himalayan mountains. The village faced Mount Makalu, an imposing, pyramid-shaped monster and the fifth-highest peak in the world. This incredible mountain was visible from every corner of the village, but I enjoyed it most in the mornings when I stepped out of our barn. Our generous hosts renovated this structure and relocated several of their animals to create an extra bedroom for my family. Every morning I ducked through the low barn doorway and stood to face the four sharp ridges of Makalu. Each morning was the same. After our second day in Mamling, I figured out how to ask our hosts for hot water. For the next ten mornings I enjoyed sipping coffee while admiring all 27,765 feet of Makalu.

On this final morning in Mamling, after enjoying my daily routine, I took a cup of coffee back into the barn for my wife Erica. She was rifling through Sheffield's suitcase, and I could tell that something was wrong. "Are you okay?" I whispered. Sheffield (2), Naomi (10), and Jack (13) were still sleeping, and we still had plenty of time before we needed to pack up. Erica stopped and faced me: "I can't find any more diapers. Do you have any in your backpack?" I shook my head. We had a 28-hour bus ride ahead of us, and Sheffield was not potty trained. "I must have miscounted the diapers when we left Kathmandu," Erica whispered. "This is the last diaper, and it needs to last us *28 hours*." She held up the wrinkled diaper as an exclamation point. As an active two-year-old, Sheffield required about seven diapers a day.

If we were traveling alone, the diaper dilemma would not have troubled us as much. Instead, we were sharing a bus with 27 college students, my professor colleague Adam, and our two missionary hosts; if Sheffield had an accident, everyone would suffer. The bus was tightly packed and there was little ventilation. Erica and I imagined the worst, but without options, we decided to save the last diaper for the ride. Until we stepped onto the bus four hours later, Sheffield would be naked from the waist down.

We shared our dilemma with some of the community leaders, and they told us that we might find diapers at a mountain pharmacy. We were still several hours away from the larger villages, and the impending disaster of a poop accident was real and unnerving. As word spread through the team about our diaper deficiency, conversations were sparked regarding diapers and culture. In many of the countries we visited on this trip, local families did not put diapers on their children. In different parts of Africa, and in the communities we visited in Latin America, many of the babies ran around sans shorts. In India and China we even saw baby pants with open crotches. Our missionary hosts in Nepal, the Baltimores, explained that by putting a diaper on Sheffield, we might actually be adding an additional cultural barrier. "Think of this as a chance to live like a Nepali family," Sandra Baltimore encouraged us as we stepped onto the bus.

With Adam, the Baltimores, and the student team now aware of our diaper crisis, Erica and I felt better. For the next ten hours, as we bounced and twisted on dirt roads through the Himalayan foothills, we took frequent stops and gave Sheffield many opportunities to jump off the bus and squat on the side of the road. He received great cheers from the team each time he made a ditch deposit on one of these breaks, and this affirmation motivated him. On some of our pitstops, when the college students were shopping for snacks, we made Sheffield walk for a while through the town. As happened so often on our international adventures, families with small children greeted us and wanted to talk. With translation help from Sandra and Robert Baltimore, these Nepali families asked a question that we heard frequently: "You brought your tiny baby to Nepal?" This question, asked in surprise, always turned into a statement of affection and celebration: "You brought your tiny baby to Nepal!" We discovered that these folks were affirmed by our trust in their community.

After ten hours on the road, we found a pharmacy with diapers.

Even many years later, this event of *the last diaper* is a favorite story in our family. While it began as a bit of a crisis, the support we received from our traveling team, as well as from the Nepali villagers all along the way, turned this potential disaster into one of our favorite travel experiences. The story of the last diaper epitomizes much of our ten years of travel as a family. We planned our adventures with care, yet we always needed to depend on our teams and the local communities in significant ways. Our four trips around the world, leading Concordia University's Around-the-World Semester program, took us far from the security of Western conveniences, and gave us valuable opportunities to experience life, culture, and family in new ways.

The stories in this collection are not part of a continuous narrative, yet each recounts a moment when we experienced the goodness of God on the shoulder of a friend. These are moments when we found ourselves needing to depend upon our team or on the community around us. These beautiful moments occurred when doubts and discomfort threatened to capsize our adventure, yet by a beautiful miracle of God, we were able to see differently, navigate obstacles, and take hold of a deeper sense of trust and understanding. In these moments we did not possess the necessary materials, knowledge, or strength, yet because of the grace of God, expressed through the strength and goodness of friends, we found the tools to continue adventuring.

John J. Norton
December 2021

INTRODUCTION

I set out to write this book many times, yet I was never satisfied with the narrative approach in each. I've landed on a very simple style—individual travel stories. These simple stories, snapshots of adventures experienced over the last ten years, seem the best way to communicate some of the beautiful things we learned while traveling as a family. These stories are personal, told from the perspective of a husband, a father of three, a professor, and a team leader.

PART 1

ATW 2010

Adam Lee, Erica, and I began to design the 2010 trip in the fall of 2009. We chose two strong campus leaders to serve as our graduate assistants: Becca Brandt and Sam Bretzmann. We interviewed and chose our team of 23 students in November of 2009. On our departure day Jack was eight years old and Naomi was six.

Student Team:

Deana Schooler	Stephen Puls
Ethan Scherch	Ben Bolognini
Aaron Bird	Martha James
Catherine Standridge	Nicole Zeffer
Shirley Dullum	Mai Vu
Kelsey Menke	Amber Watson
Amy Rosinsky	Christine Gilbert
Annmarie Utech	Alex Flores
Jessica Schober	Erik Olsen
Joanna Steinhaus	Ellie Hanson
David Garcia	Amanda Bieniek

Trip Itinerary:

Argentina—Russia—Turkey—Israel—Jordan—Egypt—Kenya—India—Indonesia—China

Argentina:
"Party in a Slum"

Favelas, pueblos jóvenes, cantegril, barrios, colonias, precarios, villas miseria. Each of these words is used in a different Latin American country to describe the same desperate place. From the favelas of Brazil to the villas miseria of Argentina, families suffer in poverty, often without electricity, clean water, or safe sewage disposal. Additionally, these families live in vulnerable social conditions, including oppressive demands from gangs, drug dealers, and pimps. In August of 2010, we met another strong group of leaders engaging the families in the villas in a very different way.

Thanks to our student Alex Flores, who completely arranged our service project in Argentina, the team connected with an amazing community leader named Lily Mocoroa. Lily started an organization called L.I.F.E. Argentina to provide support for the thousands of children living in the villas. Lily told my team that she was driven by a vision to help the children in the villas reach their educational and vocational dreams.

On our first day serving with Lily's team, we followed her into one of the villages through a small hole in a giant wall. At barely five feet tall, Lily did not duck as she stepped through the hole, yet we were soon to recognize her giant status inside the community. As we walked through narrow alleyways, carefully avoiding free-flowing sewage lines that cut through the dirt path, Lily hugged and kissed several different people. From tattooed gang members to pregnant mothers to tiny children kicking balls of socks or trash, everyone seemed to know and love Lily. They greeted her from the doorways of scrap metal houses, some handing her babies, others asking her to pray for their sick relatives.

When we arrived at the villa community center where Lily directed her programs, the children flocked around her. On our first day in this community,

Lily introduced us to some of her leaders, and they put us to work in various capacities. Some of us were assigned to the *soccer field*, which was the cement foundation for a large building that was never constructed. Others were sent into the community center building to gather tables and chairs, and to set up an art center near the *soccer field*. A third group was formed to look out for the older boys whom we would take to an indoor soccer facility that Lily often rented for part of the afternoon.

The art center filled up immediately, and my six-year-old daughter Naomi worked with our team of college girls to prepare paints and different articles for an art project. As the kids from the neighborhood arrived, they were welcomed and invited to join our team in the project.

The *soccer field* was a bit less organized–some of the kids playing tag, others just running around with a soccer ball. Some of my students gave piggy-back rides in this area, and I can still see Brock Powell, a giant at six foot three, bending over to allow four small kids to get on his back at one time. My wife Erica drifted toward a group of moms at the edge of the *soccer field*, and within minutes she was holding and snuggling little babies.

The older boys sauntered up in the midst of all this activity, playing it cool on the perimeter. Lily spotted one she knew and called him over. He smiled when she gave him a big hug in front of all his buddies, and he looked into her eyes as she spoke. She told him about the indoor field that she'd rented, and he nodded. When she waved me over, she indicated that this young man, Eduardo, knew the way to the field and that he would be our guide.

We followed Eduardo and his five friends through a maze of narrow alleys and fences, all lined by wooden or sheet-metal shacks. The villas date back to the 1930s when a military coup removed elected president Hipolito Irigoyen from office. While President Irigoyen was part of a controversial faction, the coup marked an end to 68 years of constitutional order. The breaking of Argentina's constitution opened the door to tumultuous election fraud and a destructive back-and-forth movement between dictatorship and democracy. Tragically, the villas continue to grow, and current records indicate that there are more than two million people living in Argentina's villas without sanitation systems, clean water, or electricity. Eduardo led us beneath tangled masses of low-hanging electrical lines and over several tributaries of sewage that meandered lazily through the slum. As we walked, I noticed that Eduardo's group soon doubled, and by the time we reached the indoor facility, it had tripled.

We formed three teams, each an even mix of locals and visitors. Eduardo had to explain this team formation to his friends, as it was clear that many of them would have preferred to just play Argentina vs. USA. While we had a few very good athletes on our Concordia team, we did not have the numbers to compete with these guys. This mixing of teams was likely to have been an order from Lily that Eduardo was careful to honor, and it ended up allowing several of us to bond quickly. We played a king-of-the-hill style format, where the first goal sent the losing team to the benches and brought the benched team into the game. It was fast paced and fun, but every time I received a pass the ball was stolen immediately. I was soon relegated to be goalie, which is always a bad sign. While I allowed many shots into the goal, the few that I managed to save earned me some enthusiastic back slaps from my Argentine teammates. My son Jack was on my team, and he was also relegated to the defensive portion of the field. Unlike me, Jack seemed to succeed every time the ball entered his side of the pitch. He blocked shots, interrupted fast-breaks, and often sent the ball sailing to the far end of the field to the enthusiastic praise of our teammates.

On our way back from the indoor field we were covered in sweat, and little Jack was also covered by the hands and arms of Eduardo and his friends. They were all over Jack, hugging him in an encouraging way. When we approached the community center, Lily was holding a small birthday cake. She waved us into the building, and in the front of the room we saw a pile of brightly wrapped presents stacked on a table. She pulled me aside and said, "The present we give each of these kids may be the only present they receive for their birthday. These are simple gifts, but the kids really love them. It would mean a lot to them if you helped me hand them out." I agreed, and Lily started the festivities with a round of "Feliz Cumpleaños!"

Eight children had birthdays that day, and each time Lily invited one up to the front of the room, she said a few encouraging words about them. I handed each child a present and gave each a hug. The last child Lily invited up was Eduardo, and those of us who had played soccer with him shouted with extra enthusiasm and patted him on the back. I handed Eduardo his gift, gave him a hug, and told him that he and Jack had the same birthday. He beamed and jumped over to where Jack was sitting.

After we cleaned up the community center and said our farewells to the leaders and the kids, we started walking back to our bus. On our way we heard someone shouting. It was Eduardo running after us. "Jack, Jack!" he shouted. When he came up, he was out of breath and speaking Spanish too quickly for me to understand. Lily walked up and translated, "He wants Jack to have part of his birthday present. He noticed that Jack was the only kid in the room who didn't get a present, and he wants to share his gift." A sudden pool of tears formed in my eyes. I wanted to refuse, but I knew that Eduardo felt a real connection with Jack. The boys hugged, I gave Eduardo a squeeze, and we said goodbye. Eduardo waved to us as our bus pulled away, his face beaming.

As I waved back to Eduardo I strained to focus, but my eyes would not clear. We came to serve this community. We had come to give gifts, to lead games, and to be an encouragement. These kids were living in desperate conditions, daily threatened by predatory forces. Yet, at the art table and in the soccer games, these kids had blessed and encouraged us. At the birthday party I handed out presents, but Eduardo handed a present to my son, wanting him to feel special, included, and loved.

Russia: "Picking Potatoes and Making Friends"

Our first steps in Vladimir, a 12th-century Russian city, involved a panicked rush to get Naomi to a garden planter. After she vomited a few times, Naomi looked up at me with fear in her eyes, "Daddy, my stomach really hurts." No parent likes to hear these words from their child, but the concern is deepened when home and the security of a familiar medical system are more than four thousand miles away. After a 28-hour travel day from Argentina, through New York, Helsinki, and into Moscow, which involved three flights and a long bus ride, my six-year-old daughter Naomi staggered off our bus with intense nausea. I held her hair as she leaned over a patch of bushes near the side of the road. Was this too much for her? Did I stretch my six-year-old too far with this giant trip? I whispered a prayer near her ear. We sat down on the curb near the planter and watched our team unload the bus. We had arrived at our destination, a church compound which our hosts called home base. As the last backpacks were removed from the bus, Naomi took my hand and stood up, "Ok, let's go in. I'm feeling better." This simple moment of struggle and answered prayer would return to us in some unexpected ways through the remainder of the trip.

The next day, we worked alongside our missionary hosts, Paul and Sergei of Mercy Ministries. By faith these two men and their families followed the call of God to be a part of a massive rescue operation in Vladimir. The focus of this operation was a desperate orphan population, boys and girls who were wasting away in unhealthy and overpopulated state-run homes. Mercy Ministries focused on children's homes notorious for abuse and neglect. "When we started this work," Sergei explained, "the task seemed too difficult, too dark. But as we began to pray, to seek God for a way forward, He opened many doors. We focus on one child, one conversation, and one day at a time in this ministry." Sergei's comments took me back to the prior night, sitting with Naomi, feeling overwhelmed, and then seeing God bring a miraculous level of comfort and confidence.

Paul and Sergei took us to one of their most challenging orphanages, where our team dramatized a Bible story, sang songs, and played games with the kids. Many of the young children joined us for songs and for games, and it was fun to see them light up after hearing the story of God's faithful love for Daniel, who miraculously survived an evening in a lion's den. We spoke about the fact that God is always with us, no matter how desperate things may seem. After stories, games, and music, we formed teams to complete chores with the boys and girls.

Some of us joined the teens to harvest potatoes, others weeded in the gardens, and others swept the sidewalks all over the 15-acre campus. I joined the potato harvesting team, and the Russian students laughed when I squatted closely behind them, watching their techniques and asking them questions about their potato-hunting methods. I had no idea what I was doing, and the boys and girls kindly coached me about how best to dig up the potatoes. As we dug, we shared stories and told jokes in broken English and Russian phrases. While digging, I remember my student Stephen Puls holding up a tiny, mud-covered potato and shouting, "kartoshka!" The Russian students fell over in laughter, one of them pressing two small pebbles into the top of the potato for a finishing touch. A *kartoshka* is a Russian pastry made in every bakery from the leftover frostings, icings, and fillings. The bakers shake some cocoa into the mix and press the pieces into the shape of potatoes. After 90 minutes of digging, our buckets were full, and we were covered in sweat. We kept a few *kartoshkas* to take back to the other students and returned to the group with our faces and hands streaked with dirt. The fake treats ignited more laughter back at the soccer field in the center of the orphanage grounds.

Conversations continued on the side of the soccer field, mostly inspired by silly things the players were doing in the game. Some of my students were very skilled soccer players, as were many of the Russian kids. They each seemed to want to one-up each other with fancy moves and tricks. It was all very good-spirited, yet the language barrier frustrated my hopes to engage the boys around me with anything deep or personal. I wanted to ask and to share many things, yet we were relegated to simple jokes, broken language phrases, and dramatic gestures.

On our drive back to the church compound, I was quiet. Like he had read my mind, Paul turned to me with a gleaming smile: "Do you understand why that visit was so important?" I said no, and he put his hand on my shoulder, "John, those kids have been abandoned by everyone in their lives. They are out here in the middle of nowhere, and they know that their prospects for good jobs are slim after high school graduation. While the Russians may claim not to care about America, they truly love all things American."

Paul went on to describe the significance of simple expressions of love. He compared his missionary calling to that of a builder, connecting each gift of kindness to the raising of a wall or the sealing of a roof. He patted my shoulder and thanked Adam and I for bringing such a great team to support him. He looked back at the orphanage in the distance: "God is building something here, and I am so happy to be a part of His construction of faith in the lives of the lost, the broken, and the lonely."

Paul's words struck my ears with great force. I was seeing only the surface of things; Paul was seeing with spiritual eyes. He discerned a deeper reality that I completely overlooked. Just as Naomi's heart had been filled with new faith when God healed her on our first night in Vladimir, the Lord did something powerful in my heart as I listened to Paul and reflected on our time with the young people at the orphanage. Our Heavenly Father uses the simplest offerings of humor, attention, and conversation to tear down walls of fear, depression, and loneliness. I knew by faith that God could take our simple gift of time and kindness and use it to build hope in the hearts and minds of children. These works we do by faith are not measured by worldly scales.

Jordan: "Learning to Read and Write, Again"

When I told my sister about our trip to Egypt and Jordan, her face blanched: "You're not going to use the ferry station at Taba are you?" Natalie lived in the Middle East for many years as a missionary, and she knew the area well. At that moment, I think she forgot that my children were listening. "It's very dangerous," she pressed, "I've seen so many fights there, and people get mugged or stabbed or assaulted." I explained that it was too late to change plans, and that our group of 30 would stay close and be alert. The ferry she described ran between Egypt and Jordan. Our host in Jordan warned us that the ferries often ran very late; trips scheduled for noon may not leave until 6:00pm. He did not say anything about stabbings or assaults.

Eight weeks later, we led our team through the Sinai Peninsula. We stayed at a Bedouin camp, complete with open-sided tents, colorful pillows, red and yellow rugs, and gallons of apple tea. Our Bedouin hosts convinced us to hike Mount Sinai one afternoon and to sleep at the summit–this was the only way to guarantee a good view of the sunrise. Our experience hiking Sinai, although physically challenging, served to bring us together as a team in a powerful way. Rocky mountains surround Sinai on every side, and some have compared the view to *an ocean of petrified waves*. The climb required the team to work together, especially for the final stretch, which involved bouldering the 3,750 *Steps of Repentance*. We finished the hike after dark, made camp, and ate a picnic dinner at the edge of the summit. After dinner we sang worship songs under a sky of bright stars.

The next day, after a knee-cracking descent and a long drive through the desert, our bus neared the Taba station. Our driver reached over and put his hand on my arm. "Professor," he whispered, "you know that tensions can run high at the station. It is due to mismanagement, and people get very pushy and aggressive. Keep your team close, and watch carefully for your children, especially." He lifted his hand and squeezed my shoulder, "Jordan is a crazy place. I think you should stay in Egypt." He smiled and slapped my shoulder, trying to reassure me, I think.

Taba Ferry Station is a giant warehouse with hundreds of airplane-style seats bolted in parallel rows to the cement floor. The place was packed and loud; boisterous conversations bounced from the cement floor to the slanted metal roof high above us. All of the travelers around us wore traditional Islamic robes, *thawbs* on the men and *hijabs* on the women. We located a few open rows of seats at one end of the station. Some of the team settled into reading or writing, while others broke into card games, seemingly unmoved by the tension I felt in the warehouse. I found a seat that allowed me to keep an eye on our group, on my family, and on what seemed like an unstable social climate. An hour passed without an incident, so I opened my notebook and started prepping for my next linguistics class. The lesson focused on the foundations of the Arabic language, but it also included writing Arabic letters and simple phrases.

While writing, I often heard groups of men shouting in different parts of the station. At one point, when I heard a loud scream at the other side of the terminal, I noticed that a group of men in thawbs was gathering behind me. They were pointing at me and whispering. When I turned to face them, one man stepped forward. I jumped to my feet, not knowing what to expect, and my sudden movement made him jump back, place a hand on his heart, and throw his head back in laughter. "My friend," he said, "you startled me!" He stepped forward and pointed to my notebook. "We noticed that you are writing in Arabic." He gestured to the men behind him, and five others approached, close enough to place a gentle hand on my shoulder. Although my nerves calmed, a few of my students were alarmed and stepped up beside me.

As the men gathered closer, I held up my Arabic workbook and said, "Yes, I am trying to learn to write the Arabic alphabet." The men smiled and pressed in, the stifling heat of the terminal rising another ten degrees. I was surprised with their interest, and I could tell that they were kind people. "This is not right," said the man who had spoken first. He pointed at my notebook and at my rendering of the letter A, *alif*, at the top of the page. "Your letters are very bad, very bad," he said. I chuckled at his honesty, and I handed him my notebook. "Please help me," I said, and he took my pen, and showed me how to properly compose the letter. I followed his method, and the other men voiced praise.

While I drew a few successful alifs, a man from the middle of the crowd pushed forward and put his hand on my shoulder, "Why are you here in Egypt? Is this your family?" He pointed to Jack and Naomi, who were lying on their backpacks near my feet, asleep. I said yes, and indicated with a wave that I was leading an entire group of Americans. I told them how our trip involved learning Egyptian and Jordanian history and literature, as well as the basics of Arabic. The group of men smiled and nodded approval. With a blend of astonishment and praise, one man said, "You brought your family to Egypt!" His exclamation reminded me of what many of our friends had said before our departure, yet they said it with worry and alarm. I saw the value of our journey through this Egyptian man's eyes.

The group of men stayed with us for over an hour, providing some language tips, and teaching me to write my name and several other words and phrases. Our discussion about language led to a conversation about culture, American politics, and about the tensions in the Middle East. By the end of our hour together we were exchanging emails, becoming Facebook friends, and hugging. It was an interaction that taught me to withhold judgment, to extend the benefit of the doubt, and to stay open to others, even when my fears and insecurities tell me to hide.

Egypt: "Surrounded by an Unexpected Kindness"

The traffic through Cairo was intense, taxi drivers yelling at pedestrians, pedestrians yelling at buses. Erica, Jack, Naomi, and I were sweating in a yellow cab in the middle of a river of cars, all honking and swerving toward the Opera Square. After sitting still for ten minutes, I recognized the Opera house in the distance and suggested to Erica that we walk the rest of the way. She agreed, and we signaled to the driver. He nodded and pointed to the meter, five Egyptian pounds, the equivalent of 50 cents in United States currency. Not thinking clearly, I pulled a five US dollar out of my wallet. As soon as I lifted the bill up, I realized my error, and switched it for a ten pound Egyptian bill.

The taxi driver smelled an opportunity, and pointed at the five dollar bill I'd just returned to my wallet. I shook my head and pushed the ten pound Egyptian note toward him. Without warning he raised his voice in sudden protest, spit flying into my sunglasses, and demanded I give him five US dollar for our half-mile trip. I placed the Egyptian bill on his hood—he would not accept it—and I turned to Erica. "I think this guy just lost his mind," I said. Erica nodded and led the kids away from the car and toward the sidewalk.

The taxi driver was persistent and he followed close, yelling at the back of my head. I instructed Erica to find refuge inside of a store, and I turned to face the raging man. I lifted my hands, extending them toward his chest, just in case he decided to take a swing at me. His red face was spitting and fuming, and his hands were flying wildly between us. I glanced left and right for some help, a policeman, or even a friendly face.

An hour prior to this encounter, I was crouching and shuffling through a dark, narrow passageway into the Great Pyramid of Giza. I am not usually claustrophobic, but this tight, hot space made me very uncomfortable. At about 30 feet into the pyramid, the line stopped. With my head bent over and sweat pouring down my face, I was about to turn around and join the stream of departing tourists. It must have been the twist in my posture that made an Australian man pat me on the shoulder. He was walking in the exit line and said, "Hey mate, the ceiling opens up and the tunnel gets bigger in about 20 meters. It's definitely worth seeing." I knew I could do 20 more meters, so I kept shuffling forward. The ceiling did indeed open up, and the adventure was worth the strain. My experience as a traveler has led me to depend on fellow travelers. My experience as a traveler has led me to believe that friends emerge in some of the most unexpected moments, and before panicking, it is always worth looking around for help.

As I faced the Egyptian taxi driver, my hands prepared to block his fists, a group of Egyptian men gathered around me. For a moment I thought that this was the end; my death would be at the hands of an angry Egyptian mob, all because I was too cheap to give the driver five dollars. One of the Egyptian men in the crowd put his hand on my shoulder. I tensed and spun to face him, my hands still raised. He smiled at me, and raised his own hands to show he meant no harm. He said, "Hi, what is the problem? Can I help you?" His English was perfect. I turned back to face the taxi driver, still screaming and leaning toward me. "This taxi driver is trying to cheat me." The taxi driver raged at my accusation, but I could not understand what he was yelling.

The calm friend at my side put his hand on my shoulder, gently but firmly pulling me behind him. He said "Okay," and yelled something to the men around him. They nodded and circled up around the taxi driver. The crowd of men began to move away from me; they were pushing the taxi driver back to his car. My calm friend continued to smile, stayed with me for a moment longer and said, "This man is crazy. We will take care of him. Welcome to Egypt! We are really happy that you visited! And sorry for the trouble!"

I stood on the sidewalk for a moment longer, staring at the men as they led the taxi driver away. When I turned to walk back to our hostel, I found Erica and the kids sitting on a bench holding ice-cream cones.

Kenya: "The Rescued Turned Rescuer"

I met Douglas in a church in Nairobi. He served as the lead singer of a rock band called "The Conquerors." He and his band performed all over the city—birthday parties, church events, and music festivals. "We love playing music," Douglas explained, "but our goal is to share the hope of Christ. We have all been rescued, and now we are called to be conquerors—conquerors of depression, drugs, and other harmful bondage."

Douglas told me about the glue-sniffing epidemic among street kids in Kawangware, one of the major slum communities near the capital city. He said, "When you sleep on the streets, it is very hard to relax. A few deep sniffs of glue, and you forget you are hungry; you can sleep anywhere." Douglas told me that kids in the slum can purchase a spoonful of glue for about seven cents. Once addicted, kids keep the glue in a small bottle at the end of their sleeve—always ready for a hit. The glue is not only hallucinatory and extremely addictive, but it has been known to cause respiratory infections and brain damage.

When I asked Douglas why there were so many homeless children in Kawangware, he said, "There is so much illness here in the slum, and so many kids lose their parents to diseases. AIDS is a big one, but there are many others. Some kids are forced out of their homes at an early age because they become financial burdens to their parents or other family members." Douglas went on to tell me about his own struggle with addiction.

Douglas grew up in a big family. He started playing guitar and singing as a child, and he and his siblings were active in sports. His parents died when he was nine years old, and everything collapsed for a while. Some of his younger brothers and sisters were taken in by relatives, but there was not enough space for Douglas. He was forced to live on the streets. He said, "I tried to avoid sniffing glue, but when you have to rummage through the trash and eat really terrible things, the glue *high* makes it easier." One afternoon Douglas met some of the church elders; they invited him to eat lunch at the Lutheran Church in the slum. He met the pastor and a few more of the church members, and the leaders took him under their care. They helped him find a safe place to sleep, and arranged for him to go to school.

The Lutheran Church served as a dynamic force in Douglas' life and in the lives of many more boys—Christ was moving, and many hurting children were being rescued from life on the streets. Douglas told me that he was deeply impacted by the church leaders, and when he entered his teen years, he began serving in the church's youth ministry. This was not an ordinary youth group. Some of the young leaders in this group walked through the slum each afternoon looking for homeless kids, or kids who looked like they were hungry. The church offered free meals each week and connected the needy with resources.

As I was talking with Douglas, I could see Jack running around the playground, laughing and playing with the other nine- and ten-year-olds. For a moment, I imagined my own son walking the streets alone, desperate and vulnerable. Douglas' story crashed through my defenses. Homelessness and drug addiction concerned me, but until that moment, I never imagined those as realities for a child like mine. In that moment, through Douglas' testimony of struggle, I saw my own son Jack rummaging for food, struggling to sleep, and searching for a place to hide.

Over the next ten days we served in the community with Douglas and his team of friends. We walked along the sewage lines and collected trash. We painted the community center where kids in the community receive tutoring. We helped families clear brush from around their homes and fixed insecure or flooded pathways. Some of us followed Douglas on a few of his weekly visits to older men and women in the community, many of whom were bedridden. It was moving to see the way that Douglas and the church community engaged the community with such compassion. Douglas had been transformed by the love of Christ through the faithful hands of the Lutheran Church, and now he was taking up the very work that helped him escape life on the streets.

On one of our last nights in Nairobi, we hosted Douglas, his band mates, and several of the other church leaders to an American-style barbeque at our team house. Many of them expressed an interest in trying a hamburger, and so we put together a big dinner and music party. They all seemed to enjoy the burgers, but the real fun started with the music. As we sang and prayed and worshiped together, Douglas' comments about being rescued and now called to be conquerors came back to me. We had both been rescued, and now, even in our weakness and doubt, even in our sin, God was using us to bring hope to those in bondage.

India:
"Over Budget
and Overwhelmed"

When Pastor Christopher asked to speak with my colleague Adam Lee and me privately in his office, a shiver of concern ran over my skin. Had our team insulted or offended one of the five Lutheran Church communities that called the Mumbai Lutheran Center home? Had we miscommunicated with Pastor Christopher in some way?

The church office was on the second floor of the Lutheran Center building, and we had to walk through a maze of bookshelves to reach Pastor Christopher's desk. We sat on metal chairs facing the pastor, and he had a white folder open in front of him with many other papers and receipts tucked inside of it. "Brothers," he began, his voice was always very soft and kind, "I have a little problem I need to speak with you about." The temperature in my face started to rise. "You were very clear with us about your team budget," he said, "and we know that you have a long trip. It has come to my attention that our cooking team, the ladies who have been making your meals, has overspent your budget." He paused here and looked down at the stack of receipts in his folder. "I want you to know, however, that I have talked with the congregations, and everyone is in agreement about pitching in to pay for these extra costs." I couldn't believe what I was hearing.

The church congregation was made up of people living all over the city. I knew from my conversations with various members that many people were living close to the poverty line. Some of the church members lived in the slums that dotted the area around the church, and yet these men and women were going to help our team pay its bills? I did not know how to respond right away, and when I looked at Adam, he had the same expression of disbelief. If we refused their gift, we ran the risk of offending them, but how could we allow them to make a sacrifice like this for us?

Adam and I thanked Pastor Christopher for the church's generosity. We explained that we had some extra money to cover some overages, and that we did not want anyone to go hungry by helping us. He smiled and said, "Oh, brothers, we are very honored to help, and we are very happy to have you as our guests." With that, Pastor Christopher stood up and walked us downstairs into the church courtyard. We only had a few more days in Mumbai, but the pastor's love and generosity, as well as the generosity of the congregation, really impacted me. What did it mean to welcome strangers into your home? What was the nature of true, sacrificial hospitality? This church taught us a profound lesson of love and generosity.

Indonesia: "Dancing without Hesitation"

After an intense two-week cultural experience in Mumbai, we traveled to the soothing rainforests of Bali. We knew this was a special place when we landed at the Denpasar airport and witnessed quiet, swaying trees amid a lush, green landscape. Our host Nicki was an American expat who found a way to stretch her retirement dollars in this island paradise. Nicki helped organize our accommodations in Ubud, and she connected our team to a wonderful non-profit organization in town called Sjaki-Tari-Us.

When Nicki gave our team a cultural orientation, she described the people in Ubud as incredibly hospitable and kindly enterprising. "While there are plenty of taxis in town," she explained, "each of the locals will offer you taxi service if they have room in their car. Even if they don't have room, the locals will sit on top of one another or stand on bumpers and running boards, in order to make room for you in their car." The locals were really fair to us, and I never heard of anyone on our team getting cheated through this unofficial taxi system. We took many memorable rides in cars that appeared full, but after some creative shuffling, there magically appeared open seats. I remember one weekday afternoon slipping into the backseat of a small sedan only to find that I was surrounded by a half dozen little Balinese beauty queens. These little girls, most likely on their way to a Hindu religious rite, wore brightly colored dresses and thick layers of makeup. They smiled at me and giggled, overjoyed to show me off to their neighbors as they transported me to the Sjaki-Tari-Us facility.

With the Sjaki-Tari-Us team we worked with children with special needs. This amazing organization made it their goal to rescue children with severe autism or Down Syndrome from Bali's brutal cultural stigmas. One stigma is related to a belief that children with special needs are part of a curse on a family. The families that believe this terrible lie keep their children hidden away from public view, some in back rooms and some in closets. The Sjaki-Tari-Us team actively promotes education in the community about the beauty and value of all children, and especially promotes the importance of education and development for children with disabilities.

As I squeezed into "family taxis" and interacted with friendly shop owners, many of whom would walk around counters or take great efforts to hug Jack and Naomi in the midst of bustling mid-day hours, it was increasingly difficult for me to imagine these folks locking away precious children with special needs. This was such a kind and affectionate culture, yet this horrific stigma continued to keep many people shackled to unhealthy views of blessings and curses. The Sjaki-Tari-Us team was changing cultural beliefs, and the organization had hard data to show that their work was helping to weaken these inhumane stigmas. Each week the Sjaki-Tari-Us team was recruiting more and more kids with special needs, hoping to provide new opportunities to a greater number of children.

It was an energetic class of kids that the Sjaki-Tari-Us leaders asked our team of 36 to help serve. Our project involved making handicrafts with the children in the program—bags, clocks, and a whole assortment of other creative pieces—items that would be sold at the annual concert and silent auction. The big event was scheduled for our final day in Bali, and the team expected over five hundred people to attend. Although we pushed hard to complete some really good products, we always took time to play and interact with the children. The Sjaki-Tari-Us team cultivated an upbeat and positive attitude at the center. Music was always playing from speakers overhead, and if a song with a fun beat started, it was not uncommon for spontaneous dance parties to break out. The children would initiate by grabbing hands and pulling others to the middle of the room. In addition to the mid-day dancing, the afternoon work session always ended with an all-team line dance. Few of the children at the center knew how to read a clock, but it seemed that they always knew when the classes were coming to an end. One or two of the children would point to the speakers, which was a signal to turn on a dance-friendly song with some good beat. We followed the kids as they pushed us into a big circle. If a member of the group was not dancing, one of the children was quick to run over and provide some motivation. Common motivational strategies included grabbing hands, spinning the non-dancer, or simply jumping and waving arms.

By the end of the day I was often tired and drenched in sweat, but it was impossible to sit down during the final line dance. There were two little girls, both with Down Syndrome, who sought me out before the final dance—first to make sure I wasn't sitting, and second to watch my creative dance moves. I remember tears filling my eyes during a few of those final dances, as I watched those incredible boys and girls light up the room, embrace and encourage each other, and dance without hesitation. There was so much to learn from those children—their love, their hope, and their joy brought a lightness to my spirit, reminding me to enjoy each precious moment.

Witnessing the shocking tension between a loving community and their horrific stigmas forced me to consider my own life and the habits I encourage in my own community. God calls us to love one another and to care for one another, yet at home my concerns revolve around my own comfort and security. I began to think of the members in my community that I directly or indirectly relegated to back rooms, or worse, to the darkened corners of my attention. Working in this Indonesian community reminded me of my own inattention to the suffering and forgotten in my own community. As we left Bali, I prayed that God would give me new eyes and a new heart for my own community back home.

China:
"Raw Fish Surprise"

Our arrival into China involved many mixed emotions. The power and the danger, the historic oppression and the secretive nature of China's foreign policy made me feel that I was stepping behind a veil. I wondered if our students would be welcomed and treated kindly. I wondered if my family would be watched and carefully guided by our hosts, or if we would be allowed the freedom to explore. I was also concerned about the freedoms we would be offered to worship as a team, as this was a central part of our community identity. We had been on the road for over four months, and prayer and worship sustained us as a traveling family. I wondered if our Chinese hosts would pressure us to refrain from these vital team practices.

We landed in Hong Kong and traveled across the border by bus to our host city Shenzhen. Shenzhen is a relatively new city in China, established in 1979, but it has more than six thousand years of history. Historical records dating from 1410 bear the name Shenzhen, which means that the city may have been established as early as the Ming Dynasty. Our team enjoyed visiting a few restored cultural sites, including the Nantou Ancient City and Dapeng Fortress. Many of the relics at these sites were over six hundred years old. The Hakka people, migrating to the city in the 18th century, are part of the more recent indigenous populations in Shenzhen. The city is technologically advanced, and parts of its infrastructure reminded us of Southern California.

Any sense that we were in a place of oppression or danger fell away when we met our hosts. These men and women were generous with their time and generous with their resources. Li Na was an administrator at one of the schools where we worked. She adopted our family, and she looked after us with sweet diligence. At the beginning of our first week in China she pulled me aside:

"Dr. Norton, I would like to talk with you about your schedule for the week. On any of the nights you are not having a team meeting or doing other business, my family and I would like to take you to dinner." I could not have understood the depths of Chinese hospitality if I had not experienced it. Li Na followed up with me every afternoon, "Have your plans changed for tonight? If so, we would love to take your family to our favorite restaurant."

On our fourth night in the city, we had our first dinner with Li Na, her husband Chen, and their teenage daughter. They took us to a restaurant with what Li Na described as a "very special menu." The food was prepared by chefs from Chen's native province, Guangdong. We followed Li Na and Chen to the back of the restaurant, up a private staircase, and into a small room next to the kitchen. Li Na explained, "My husband is good friends with the owner. They have brought in a very special meal for us tonight." I was excited but also nervous. I love Chinese cuisine, and I enjoy trying very different kinds of food, no matter how exotic the preparation. I worried about the two very hungry children at my side. Jack and Naomi trooped faithfully and courageously through our five-month trip, and while we had some wild meals, we always had options. Li Na and Chen ordered one special meal.

Chen spoke limited English, and until we took seats in our special room, he remained quietly reserved. His first question came as we sat down: "You like to drink? Strong drink?" I smiled and nodded, "Yes." I examined his face for humor, but found a serious stare. Taking a risk, I pointed to my flexed bicep: "I love a strong, muscular drink!" Li Na laughed, but Chen did not understand immediately. He leaned over to her for a translation, and his face lit up in delight. He threw his head back and exploded with laughter. He ordered a special rice wine that was very muscular, but also very tasty. The wine served as an excellent pairing with the first course, a salty soup that we all enjoyed with pieces of pork, some thick noodles, and a flavorful broth.

The main course came in with a flourish. Two servers carried a large, round wicker basket into the room, which they set up in the middle of our table. Chen stood and directed the servers to pour a few different oils and to scatter a few spices over the meal. Li Na explained, "The meat in the basket is raw fish, a special fish that is popular with Hakkanese people like my husband. It is prepared with a special oil and these spices. It is always presented in a woven basket, and we eat it with chopsticks and special spoons, like these." She pointed to a stack of spoons beside the wicker basket. My stomach dropped. Raw fish pieces, spices, and an assortment of oils? I was certain that Jack and Naomi would soon break into tears. How would we explain? I hid these feelings behind a smile and a friendly nod, trying to allow enthusiasm to cover my anxiety. I turned to Erica, and she smiled and nodded, too, but I knew she shared my worry.

When the attendants departed, Chen demonstrated the eating technique. I was the first to jump in, hoping my enthusiasm would encourage my kids. Jack and Naomi watched with concern. I picked up a few pieces of fish with my chopsticks, placed them on my spoon, and topped the spoon with a peanut and a few spices I did not recognize. The flavor was amazing, and before I said anything, Jack and Naomi loaded their spoons. After one bite, they roared with enthusiasm, "This is amazing!" The kids talked about this meal for months afterward. I'll never forget looking down the table at Naomi, her little arm stretched out over the wicker basket, chopsticks extended, a huge smile. She turned to me and said, "Daddy, this is amazing. I love this fish!" Li Na and Chen clapped and laughed at the delight they saw in Jack and Naomi's faces.

Chen ordered another round of drinks, and we were soon engrossed in a fun conversation about family and culture. As we emptied the basket Chen ordered another batch and another round of the wine. He stood up from his chair, lifted his glass, and said, "I want to get drunk with you tonight, my friend!" Another awkward feeling ran through my body, and I tried to think of what to say. I stood and tapped my glass to his: "To a great night and to new friends!" Chen smiled and drained three ounces of the wine. I took a sip of mine, and Li Na chimed in, "It is our custom to empty the glass in a toast." I tipped my glass back.

When we sat back down our glasses were refilled to the brim. I thanked Chen and took what felt like another risk: "You are a wonderful host, but unfortunately I cannot get drunk. My family and my team of students are counting on me to lead them through a series of lectures in the morning." Chen seemed to understand, but he stood up again, extended his glass, and said, "You are a fine American man. I am happy to be your friend. I am happy to have a fine American friend." I stood, toasted his glass, but I did not swig the contents. He looked at my glass with concern and whispered to Li Na. She responded to him in a whisper, and he smiled: "A very responsible, honorable American friend!" As we left the restaurant that night Chen ordered two more bottles of the rice wine: "These are a gift for my new American friend!"

With a box of rice wine under each arm, I leaned toward Li Na to accept a warm hug. In a quiet tone she said, "I want your team to be able to pray and read your Bibles. Feel free to lower the curtains in your team room at my school. You can sing or pray as much as you like. You are very welcome here." Li Na's quiet tone made it clear that her permissions may not have been entirely legal or supported by her public school district, but I was overwhelmed by her kindness. She and Chen wanted to walk us back to our hotel, but we insisted that we could manage the two-block distance by ourselves. This couple embraced us with an overwhelming hospitality, and their care for us continued until our very last moments in the city. While China still withheld a great sense of mystery for me at the end of our adventure, like two bright threads in a complex tapestry, compassion and generosity now took a central place in our memory of this country.

China:
"Miming toward
Friendship"

A massive steel gate, a company of guards, and a crowd of people stood between us and our host school in Shenzhen. When my eyes adjusted to the chaotic scene before us, I saw a woman waving enthusiastically and smiling at our bus. This was how we first met Li Na, the woman I described in the previous story. Li Na was a woman whose powerful personality and sharp mind served to bless my family and my team during our three-week adventure in China.

When we stepped off our bus, Li Na called the security guards and they ushered us into the school grounds. Li Na continued to wave to us, but also gestured to a giant welcome banner hung on the side of the school building, a brand-new, white, massive seven-story edifice. Li Na's enthusiasm and energy swept away any nerves I had in that moment. She exuded genuine kindness, but as she drew our team together in the courtyard of the school, she also communicated a strong sense of leadership and organization.

We were all a bit uncertain about the home-stay adventure, but after listening to Li Na's greeting, our hopes were raised. Over 100 men, women, and children began filing into the courtyard during Li Na's welcome address, and we soon found ourselves surrounded by a large crowd of smiling faces. After reviewing our schedule for the benefit of our team but also the homestay families, Li Na began calling out the names of families and pairing them with our students. Some of our students were sent off individually, while some were sent off in twos. Some left the school compound and walked to their homestays, while other students got into cars to head to their new home in Shenzhen.

When all of the students were gone, Li Na introduced Adam, Erica, and me to a man named Mr. Chen. "Mr. Chen will take you to your hotel now," Li Na explained. We bowed to Mr. Chen and after a few more confirmations, we followed him to his car. "We are very close to your hotel; it is very nice. You will like it," said Mr. Chen, his accent thick but his English clear and commanding.

Our hotel room was indeed very nice. It was a sprawling two-room suite with a big living room. The amenities were very clean and nice, and the kids were excited to count three TVs, two big couches, several chairs and sitting areas, and a beautiful Mahjong table. We stayed in some comfortable accommodations throughout our 19-week adventure, but the four of us usually tucked into a single hotel room with two queen beds. This two-room suite with two giant king-sized beds was like nothing we'd seen in five months of travel, and we were excited to be spoiled.

One of our most memorable nights in Shenzhen happened in the neighboring community of this hotel. It was Friday night, and after an exciting week of classes, banquets, and meetings, Erica and I were ready for a quiet weekend. Our host Li Na was worried about us being alone, and she offered to take us to dinner. I have never experienced hospitality at the scale that Li Na and her community of friends offered us. We politely declined, explaining that we were hoping to have a quiet night and to get to bed early. It took some insisting, but Li Na finally agreed that some relaxation would be good for us. We also convinced her that we would be fine on our own in the city for dinner.

We played some games and talked in our hotel room until hunger motivated us to take to the street for food. We walked about ten paces from the door of our hotel when I noticed that a car was following closely behind us. I turned to look, and recognized Mr. Chen. He waved, parked the car along the curb, and jumped out to greet us. "Hello professor! Ms. Li Na explained to me that you are having dinner alone tonight. I came to see if you need help. May I take you to dinner?" We explained to Mr. Chen that we were having a family dinner alone, but this idea made his face drop and his eyes trace the sidewalk in front of us. "You don't speak Chinese; how will you order food?" he asked. I wanted to explain that we'd been on the road for five months, making our way without translation through nine different countries. Instead, I expressed gratitude for his care and assured him that we would be okay. He nodded, and while uncertainty lingered on his face, he consented and drove away.

We were drawn into a bustling restaurant about 100 yards from our hotel. The manager led us to a table and asked us several quick questions in Chinese. I could tell he was asking about drinks, so I pointed at Erica and the kids and said, *shuǐ* (water) and at myself and said *pijiu* (beer). He smiled, nodded, and raced away. The menus on the table were all in Chinese, and there were no pictures. Menu pictures are vital in situations like these, but after navigating Shenzhen for seven days, we knew that tourist-friendly restaurants did not exist in this part of the city. I prepared myself for some aggressive charades.

When the waiter returned with the water and beer, I started to ask about rice, chicken, and fish dishes. The waiter looked mortified as he knew no English, and he clearly did not want to embarrass himself by trying. He called another waiter over to our table, and in just a few moments we were surrounded by five or six others. I was making no progress until I stood up and started flapping my elbows like a chicken. The waiters all broke out into laughter, and one shouted "Kǎo jī!" (Roast chicken). I had no idea if they understood, but we were so hungry that we nodded and repeated, *Kǎo jī*!

Next, I tried to explain that we wanted rice and fish—gesturing and waving, holding out my hand and trying to describe a pile of rice. The circle of waiters leaned in with puzzled expressions, but no luck. I think that the enthusiasm and joy that the first success granted us created some trust in the waiter. He waved away his co-workers and grabbed my hand. He led me through the restaurant and into the kitchen, holding my hand the whole way. He spread his hands out, inviting me to point at what I wanted. I pointed at fish swimming in a giant tank, gestured toward some bags of rice on a shelf, and opened the refrigerators. On the shelves in the refrigerator I pointed at soups and noodles. The waiter was thrilled at this success and shouted at the cooks in the kitchen. They all laughed, and a few of them smiled and patted me on the shoulder as the waiter led me back to our table.

The meal we ate that night was very good, but more memorably, it was a cultural experience of remarkable kindness and openness. Our waiter, who after further miming and non-verbal signaling, communicated that he was the manager. At the end of our meal, he treated me to a shot of baijiu, a grain-based spirit that many consider to be China's national drink. The manager probably would have walked us all the way back to our hotel if I had not insisted that we could manage on our own.

A funny follow-up event involving this restaurant took place the following Monday afternoon. My colleague Adam and I held a teaching event for the school district. We presented some of the English teaching methods that Adam developed while teaching English in Korea and China for many years. There were more than 200 teachers at this event, and at the end of it the superintendent of the district treated us to lunch. He drove us across town to the very restaurant that we had visited on Friday night. I walked beside the superintendent into the restaurant, and when the manager spotted us he came rushing over waving. He walked up to me with a big smile and started clucking like a chicken, arms flapping, and laughing—right in front of the superintendent and a group of 20 teachers.

This experience at the restaurant with this enthusiastic manager gave me a new appreciation for Chinese hospitality. Not only did this man work hard to offer my family a great meal, but he extended himself in generous friendship. The uncertain feelings I had about Chinese culture when we arrived in Shenzhen were overwhelmed by unexpected kindness and enthusiastic offers of hospitality.

PART 2

ATW 2012

The 2010 ATW Semester program was a success. We returned to campus on December 19, 2010 to a lot of enthusiasm, and the administration asked Adam and me to plan a second trip. In January of 2011 we began designing ATW 2012 to run in the fall 2012 semester. In order to meet the increased demand, we decided to take more students on this second trip.

We hired four graduate assistants in anticipation of a bigger team, and we were honored to invite Dana Burkey, Karen Carney, Josh Geisinger, and Ben Helge onto our leadership team.

Dean Timothy Preuss was scheduled to be on sabbatical during the fall 2012 semester. Because he had been such a great support to our program, it seemed ideal to have him and his wife Debbie join our leadership team, too. Tim's original role on the team would provide help with the budget and help with team management.

We interviewed and chose our team of students in October of 2011, and everything seemed to be running as planned until December. The leadership team was strong, and the students were wonderful.

On Christmas Eve morning we sat down to a family breakfast. Erica served me a pancake in the shape of a word: Baby. I looked up at her and said, "Baby Jesus?" She smiled, shook her head, and pointed to her stomach: "Baby." I jumped up and hugged her, tears streaming down my face. We had been hoping and praying for a third child for seven years, but it just didn't seem to be God's plan for us.

The unexpected pregnancy changed the leadership structure on the ATW 2012 team. I would stay home and provide logistical support as well as paper-grading support for Adam and his classes. Tim would take on a teaching role, and Adam would depend upon him to help with more direct team leadership. I joined the team to teach classes in India for two weeks in the middle of the semester. I also visited the team at the end of the trip, traveling with them in Bolivia and in Peru for three weeks. Jack joined me for the Bolivia-Peru adventure.

Leadership Team:

Adam Lee	Tim and Debbie Preuss*
Dana Burkey (GA)	Karen Carney (GA)
Josh Geisinger (GA)	Ben Helge (GA)

John Norton (home/ logistics/ visiting professor)

*The Preuss children: Lydia (17), Matt (14), and Abigail (11)

Student Team:

Alex Bagnara	Audrey Biesk
Zach Oedewaldt	Amber Arandas
Hayden Folks	Wesley Gong
Michelle Sackie	Nicole Zehnder
Alex Lange	Katryna DaCosta
Nick Duerr	Maggie Langdon
Lauren Linneman	Ellie Johnson
Zach Dean	Matthia Duryea
Alexandra Castellanos	Robyn Cornish
Howard McBride	Ellie Hanson
Seth Preuss	Kristine Allen
Mariah Neilson	Aaron Puls
Amanda Read	Trenton Semple
Lauren Shea	

Trip Itinerary:

Mongolia—China—Vietnam—Thailand—India—Ethiopia—Austria—Hungary—Bolivia—Peru

India:
"Invited into
His Suffering"

In the 1950s, in response to a city-wide epidemic and spiking unemployment in Kolkata, Mother Teresa began setting up homes and small medical clinics around the city to respond to the crisis. The original mission of her organization focused on caring for the sick and abandoned adults who were dying alone on the streets of Kolkata.

I was assigned a volunteer post at Prem Dan, a home and medical clinic for very sick men and women. My work was in the men's ward. There were two parts to this ward, the main building where the very sick lay dying, and a garden where those who were on the mend could relax and talk. In the garden there was a team of volunteers helping the men shave, and this seemed like a great place for me. I really wanted to avoid the medical ward.

I shaved at least ten men, and we were having some great conversations. It all fell apart for me when I had to return to the main building to restock my shaving supplies. When I entered the building, I set my eyes on the back wall where the fresh blades and clean towels were stored. As I walked quickly to the back wall, a man on my left lifted his arm: "Brother, can you help me." I looked down at a half-dressed man who was covered in bandages. I said, "Oh, yes, I will find someone for you." He said, "No brother, I just need to get to the bathroom. Can you help me stand?" I wanted to bolt, but there was no way out.

In the next moment I was bending down to help him. I discovered that he had very little use of his legs, and so I had to lift him over my shoulder, out of the bed, and to a walker nearby. I tried to help him manage the walker, but his weak legs required that I wrap my arms around his waist and nearly carry him into the bathroom. He asked me to help him remove the rest of his clothing and to help him get onto the toilet. This took a long time and I kept looking for a way out, because I was sure that there was better work for me to be doing elsewhere.

The man, Amir, asked me to wait for him as he went to the bathroom. Afterward he asked me to help him take a shower. I brought him buckets of water, and he managed to do most of the work himself, but his physical needs required that I stand uncomfortably close. At the end of the shower I brought him a towel and fresh clothing. I helped him dress and half-guided, half-carried him back to his bed. While we were gone, one of the other volunteers had changed out his bed sheets and everything looked really clean and nice.

I helped him back into his bed, and when he put his head onto his pillow I could tell that all that movement had really tired him out. Awkwardly, and hoping he would say "No," I asked if he needed anything else. In a very sweet, very kind voice, he said, "No, I feel good now. Brother, thank you very much." I walked back to the garden and determined never to set foot in the medical ward again. That experience, though sweet, was a bit too much, too close, too intimate. The next day, and for ten days after that, I was called upon to care for this very same man.

I am thankful to confess, glory to God, that my bad attitude finally dissipated (after the third day), and Amir and I ended up having good conversations about many simple things. I began to look forward to the work and the time with a man who soon became a friend. The words of Ephesians 2:8-10 took on new meaning for me as I cared for Amir. I realized a new complexity about what it means to be God's workmanship. I recognized something new and wonderful about what it means to step into work God prepares for each of us.

In Kolkata I was invited into another man's suffering, and at first, I failed to see this role clearly, properly. In a weird and confused way, I saw the intense hospice work beneath me. At the end of two weeks, I realized that I'd been invited into a very holy place, a simple place, but one that is intimate and profound. On my last day as I lifted the clean white sheets over Amir's tired body, he said, "Brother, thank you very much. See you tomorrow." I had to take a quick, deep breath in order to hold back a sudden flood of emotion. I told Amir that this was my last day with him. He turned to face me, our eyes locked, and then he thanked me, again. He put his head on the pillow, and closed his eyes.

May God give us eyes to see the simple works of love that He has created for us to do each day. May we have willing hearts, knowing and trusting that even the simplest acts of love that God invites us to perform, may in fact be sacred spaces where our own hearts may be softened and our vision cleared.

Bolivia: "The Road of Life and Death"

When my son Jack (11) and I landed in La Paz in the fall of 2012, the weight of responsibility I felt as a team leader was only matched by the unsettling weight of altitude sickness. At 13,300 feet, the El Alto International Airport is the highest international airport in the world. Protected from acclimation in the pressurized airplane, our bodies were still operating at the take-off elevation of Los Angeles (three hundred feet). Standing in the immigration line, I felt the altitude like a 50-pound sandbag on each of my shoulders. Jack and I were dizzy, and soon after we passed through the terminal, a sickening wave of nausea swept over us.

When we met our missionary host Philip Kittleson, he gave us some coca leaves and said, "Some people use these leaves to make cocaine, but in their natural form they are very helpful for combating altitude sickness." Philip must have seen the concern in my eyes: "Coca leaves must be cooked with battery acid, gasoline, cement, ammonia, and many other chemicals to create cocaine. God gave this plant to the people of this region; it is a wonderful gift. One small property of the plan has been hijacked by criminals." The leaves were helpful to us, and the altitude sickness soon passed. I still felt a heavy weight of responsibility.

After three days in La Paz our plan was to take our team of university students to Philip's hometown, Caranavi. Our journey to Caranavi involved a 43-mile journey down the infamous *La Carretera de la Muerte* (The Death Road). This narrow mountain road connected La Paz with the Yungas province. In Caranavi we planned to lead a Vacation Bible School for a small Nazarene church. Before I left home, I made the mistake of looking up videos of bus accidents on this road. Recent statistics claimed that more than three hundred drivers lost their lives on this road every year. The mix of avalanches, drunk driving, and extremely sheer cliffs made for a deadly cocktail.

As we made our way down the mountain, Philip sat beside Jack and me. He told us detailed horror stories about his 30-years of experience traversing *The Death Road*. Philip explained that there were times when he was a boy that he and his father approached accidents on the road. "Some of the accidents were fatal," he explained, "but others just sent people off the road and down onto tiny ledges on the cliffside. Some of these ledges hang over more than a two thousand-foot sheer drop; it's really quite amazing." Jack looked at Philip and then back at me; I could tell that he was growing worried. "Don't worry Jack," said Philip, "I like to call this "The Life Road," because without it my father would not have been able to establish more than a dozen churches and Christian ministries in the valley below. People have lost their lives traveling this road recklessly, but when God sends us down, we travel thoughtfully and we bring a message of life!" With that, Philip jumped to his feet and shouted, "Let's get on the roof, the view on this part of the road is amazing!"

Philip asked the bus driver to pull over to the side of the road, and half of the team climbed onto the roof of the bus. We were now about half way down the mountain, and while the sheer cliff on our left was disturbing, I had a growing sense of peace and confidence. Philip's faith and courage were contagious, and he told stories about God's amazing grace and protection to those of us sitting around him.

One story involved a time when the drug lords of Caranavi surrounded the radio station where Philip's father was preaching the Gospel and also encouraging the people to stand against the city's drug culture. Because Philip's father had a significant influence in the city, his regular radio broadcasts not only led many to Christian faith, but they damaged the drug trade. He encouraged families to refuse selling coca leaves to the known drug dealers, and to refuse to take part in the processing of cocaine, which was a very profitable family business for many in the valley.

The drug lords were armed with rifles, they surrounded the radio station, and demanded that Mr. Kittleson come out. Knowing the drug lords were merciless killers, Philip's father refused their demands and instructed Philip and their broadcasting team to huddle in the middle of the station and pray. Bullets soon flew through the building, yet no one inside was hit. After being held inside for more than 24 hours, government militia arrived to clear out the gang members. "My father continued to preach on that radio," Philip explained, "and many people came to faith as they saw him risk his life to preach the truth."

After listening to Philip's stories, I felt faith growing in my heart. Jack and I hung on his words. When we were in Caranavi we followed him around, asking questions, and just soaking up the lessons he would share about his experiences in ministry. There was something different about Philip Kittelson, something I had never seen in any Christian. He had a powerful sense of confidence, because he knew that God was with him.

The weight of altitude sickness did not last long, and as I watched Philip Kittelson lead and instruct my team of college students, I soon felt the weight of responsibility leave my shoulders, too. We were in the hands of a mighty man of God, one who had been tested in the fires of extreme oppression and violent persecution. I felt blessed to be able to meet Philip and to hear the testimony of God's grace and power in his life. I love the way God uses the fellowship of those who have traveled ahead of us on the road of faith, *The Life Road*, to encourage us, to embolden us, and to free us.

PART 3

ATW 2014

Although I was disappointed not to travel for all 17 weeks with the ATW 2012 team, it was a great joy to be able to visit that wonderful team twice. The ATW 2012 semester program was another success, and when this team hit the campus in the spring semester of 2013, they ignited a fire. Interest for the program shot to an all-time high, and Adam and I started wondering if the program would soon be running every fall instead of on the every-other-year model.

Preparations for the third ATW Semester began in January of 2013.

Leadership Team:

Adam Lee	John and Erica Norton*
Ellie Hanson (GA)	Alex Lange (GA)
Seth Preuss (GA)	Joanna Steinhaus (GA)

*The Norton children: Jack (12), Naomi (10), Sheffield (1)

Student Team:

Jacob Mueller	Elaine Sanchez
Zach de Vos	Kenneth Reyes
Kristen Maxwell	Noah Menke
Taylor Quijada	Sarah Taylor
Jared Martin	Hayden Killeen
Madeline Upchurch	Angela Duerr
Nicholas Bedell	Quincy Koll
April Hall	Camila Rebollo

Ryan Buuck Shara Leehey

Jessica Schrank Gianna Kozel

Steven McCarthy Jordan Buuck

Lydia Preuss Rachel Blair

Abigail Bretzmann Taylor Doornbos

Ryan Fink Abigail Lozano

Trip Itinerary:

Brazil—Paraguay—South Africa—Turkey—Hungary—Romania—Nepal—India—Thailand—Cambodia—South Korea

Brazil:
"Look at Me
and Breathe"

On a grassy hillside framed by Brazilian pine, a team of 28 students sat facing professor Tony Vezner. "Let's start with a drill," he said, "This is called face-to-face breathing." As the title suggests, the drill required that two students stand face to face with their eyes locked together. They were instructed to breathe normally and to hold a conversation with their faces awkwardly close together. In the first few days of practicing this drill, most of the students could not hold their position, but instead allowed their discomfort to break off eye contact and to fall into laughter. In order to encourage some of the more embarrassed members of the team with the drill, Tony created some strategic pairings. Some of the shyer students were paired with those who were more comfortable. As I walked around the class, observing some of the pairings, I heard some of the students in gentle tones saying, "Look at me and breathe." This drill created a comfort between team members that would soon prove important for much different purposes than interactive class discussion.

In addition to bonding over challenging acting drills and influential Brazilian literature, the students began connecting through service. We worked with Paul and Becky Abel, an American missionary couple. The Abels arrived in Curitiba in 1985, and in addition to establishing four churches, they developed the ARCA Bible Camp—our home base for two weeks. Curitiba is the capital of the southern Brazilian state of Parana, and famous for being one of the greenest cities on Earth. The Abels designed their camp in a way that matched the city, green and lush.

Paul and Becky broke our group into several mini-teams and sent us all around the camp and the town to do various acts of service. Some of us formed a painting crew that accomplished a variety of jobs for neighbors, others helped an elderly woman clean out her yard and clear the paths in her garden. Some teams were sent into town to serve as English tutors at a language school, and others pulled weeds, mowed lawns, and helped clean various parts of the camp. In the late afternoons when our jobs were completed, the Abels invited us to enjoy the camp amenities: playing basketball in the gym, playing human foosball, riding the giant zipline, riding their pet donkey, balancing on the slackline, and playing Ultimate Frisbee. The camp was surrounded on one side by a beautiful forest, and many of us enjoyed taking walks and exploring the countryside.

At the end of our first week, Paul Abel had a special job for one of our mini-teams. Twelve students would travel with Paul in the camp bus to a remote village in the countryside. They would do some minor construction work on a friend's property. The man they were to help had some physical limitations, and the extra hands would be a massive blessing.

My mini-team was scheduled at the same time to serve at the language school in town. Our work at the school went really well, and the students were enthusiastic to learn and to engage. Part of the English curriculum that we were assigned to cover involved a discussion about American culture. We talked about everything from the Pilgrims to rock and roll to the Christian faith. The Brazilian students were intrigued by how *religious* our team seemed to be, and many of our conversations returned to the blessing of walking with Christ as Savior and friend. This concept seemed to intrigue many of the students, and we promised to follow up with more questions at the English camp that we would host the next week at the Abel property.

As we were leaving the language school the sun was starting to set, and the Abels' son Mafu got a phone call. His face turned very serious and he spoke rapidly into the receiver. He motioned to Erica and me, and we followed him away from the group of students. Mafu explained that Paul and the students who traveled into the countryside had been in an accident. "The dirt road gave out and the bus flipped," Mafu said, "some of the students are injured, and they are on their way to the hospital." Adam, Erica, and I made a plan that involved getting the students from our language team back to the camp. Adam, Tony, and Erica would gather the students together there, and I would travel with Mafu to the hospital.

When we arrived at the hospital, I was assured that the students were not seriously injured, and I was required to wait in the lobby for about an hour. During that time I called Tim Preuss, my supervisor back at Concordia. He snapped into action and lined up all the necessary insurance pieces back on campus. Within the hour Tim faxed and emailed the necessary paperwork to the Curitiba hospital, and everything was in order. When I was finally allowed to see the students, some of my concerns dissipated when I heard distinct and familiar tones of laughter floating down the hallway. My students were in one big room, three sitting up and one laying flat, all on gurneys. They greeted me with a shout, and started recapping the event for me right away.

They explained that they were on their way back when the side of the dirt road collapsed. The bus slid off the road and tipped over onto its side. Some of the windows shattered and the students were thrown to one side of the bus. The experience was terrifying, and they described the difficulty of climbing up and out of the broken windows. One of the students had a very sore shoulder, and she had to be helped out of the window by a few of the young men. "When we got out of the bus, we were all really disoriented and unsure about what to do," one student explained. Another added, "We were in shock, and a few of us just started doing the breathing activity that Professor Vezner had taught us." The students smiled as they thought about the incident and the panic they felt after getting out of the bus. "We looked into each other's eyes, and controlled our breathing—just like in Professor Vezner's class," one student explained, "and then we started to pray."

After another two hours, the students were released from the hospital, the tests showing no signs of serious injury. The primary damage was in student confidence, and although they managed to laugh together, the students were shaken up. We returned to the camp very late into the evening, and the other team members had waited up for us. The hospital patients were met with shouts of welcome, tears, and hugs. The emotions were heavy that night, and we stayed up together for hours singing worship songs and talking. In the midst of the tears, a powerful sense of comfort rested on the team that evening as Noah and Hayden played praise songs on their guitars. The presence of the Lord was palpable that night, as He seemed to be directing our eyes to his own, reminding us to breathe, and ensuring us that he was near.

Paraguay: "Four Feet Wide and Six Feet Deep"

Luis led us to the playground and said, "We need a few of you to dig some holes around this play structure." He pointed to a colorful assembly of slides and monkey bars and swings. We were in Tobati, a small town about two hours east of the capital city of Asuncion. A large percentage of the homes in Tobati lack running water and electricity. Most of the men and older boys in the city work in brick factories. We learned that the daily school sessions in Tobati are three hours long, allowing plenty of time for children to work in the factories.

At 9:00am it was already hot, and as we toured the Su Refugio facility, our hosts Luis and his wife Kendra reminded us to drink a lot of water. Luis explained that all of the camp's water faucets were connected to very good, clean water, drawn from a deep, artesian well. The water had been tested, and unlike much of the tap water in Paraguay, the Su Refugio water was very clean and safe.

Luis and Kendra broke our team into three groups: one digging crew on the playground, one painting crew in the dormitory, and one cooking and food-service crew in the kitchen. Jack and I joined the digging crew, and to our dismay the ground was not only very hard, but the holes needed to be very, very deep. With shovels in hand we followed Luis' instructions. "The holes need to be four feet wide and six feet deep," he explained. He carved nine big x's in the dirt all around the playground equipment. We had shovels and pickaxes, but after the first few swings of each, it seemed that the ground would not give way. The shovels scratched the hard pack, and the pickaxes bounced.

Luis could see the frustration rising in our faces, and he gathered us together. "You know," he said, "the sun beats on this play structure every afternoon. It gets so hot that we cannot allow the children to play on it. These little ones love these slides and toys, and they are really heartbroken when they are required to stay inside all day." Luis explained that nine giant posts were being delivered and would be installed by a team from the States that would arrive the week after our departure. Luis gave us vision for the work our team was contributing to, we felt some energy rising.

God was doing something special here at Su Refugio, and even in our first few hours in the camp, we could all feel it and see it. Our team was just one small part of a bigger plan for this campus and for the city of Tobati. Luis and Kendra told us about the growing population of homeless children in this region of Paraguay, and hundreds of these children would be able to receive two meals each day here at Su Refugio. Some of the children came to the campus each day to eat, others lived in the dormitories full time, and others were part of the Su Refugio school. All of them heard about the love of Jesus Christ when they visited, and the mission of the organization was to share Christ's love with the entire city.

Armed with this insight, we took up the pickaxes again, and started breaking into the hard, packed soil. One of my students, Steve McCarthy, led us in some funny camp songs as our sweat poured out onto the playground. Hundreds of swings took us into the late morning, and we started to see some progress. When we quit at noon we had five holes, four feet wide, and about six inches deep! We ate lunch with the children from the city, and then returned to our campground for classes. We stayed at Kavaju Camp, a very simple camp with bunks and an open-air meeting hall. It was a beautiful site, built around the base of a rocky mountain.

On our second day at Su Refugio the temperatures soared into the nineties, and as the sweat poured off of us, the ground began to give way. We found new methods for breaking up the soil, and we managed to get all nine of the holes dug out that day. Six feet deep and four feet wide, the project that seemed impossible the day before was complete. We let out a collective shout when the final hole was dug. We all took turns hammering at the final hole, and the last few swings were made to the accompaniment of songs and loud cheering.

When Luis came by to check on us, he looked at the giant holes and lifted his arms in victory. "Guys," he said smiling, "this was supposed to take you at least ten days." We cheered some more, and Luis' smile faded: "I need to think of some more projects for you." The guys gathered up the supplies, and Adam and I walked with Luis back toward his office. We explained to him that we were very flexible. "Perhaps there is something in town that we could do for some of the families in the church," Adam offered. Luis' stopped and his eyebrows lifted: "How about some door-to-door evangelism?" This suggestion made my smile disappear, and I started to feel very uncomfortable.

While I am not a shy person, the idea of door-to-door evangelism made me think of the religious door-knockers I always try to avoid in my own neighborhood. The Lord would need to take a pickaxe to my reservations if I hoped to engage this project with much enthusiasm. Before I tried to suggest some other projects on the Su Refugio campus, Luis added, "The people in the town would love to be visited by Americans. Many of them are very poor and very lonely." This was the first swing of the axe on my reservations, and we agreed to help in any way Luis thought we could bless the community.

We explained the new evangelism project to the team that evening at Kavaju Camp. I could see discomfort break out on many faces. I confessed my own sense of unease, but I also told the students what Luis had said about the lonely men and women we'd be visiting. We prayed together as a team, asking God to give us courage and to show us how to be a blessing. As I saw the college students rally, I could feel another crack of the axe on my reservations.

The evangelism teams were small groups of three or four, and we each had a translator. Luis and Kendra explained the culturally appropriate way of approaching the homes. "You stand at the edge of their property," said Kendra, "and you clap two or three times." She explained that the clap was like a knock, but because so many of the homes were surrounded by fences, this was the safest and most acceptable way to engage the homeowners.

Naomi and I teamed up with Taylor Quijada and Kendra, and we set off down the street. There was a woman Kendra knew who was always home. She was a widow, but she cared for several older children and a few babies. On the way to this woman's house Kendra pointed at a few different homes, and we took turns clapping. At the first house our clapping signaled a giant dog who lunged at the fence, snarling.

At the second house an older man came out to meet us, and he had many questions about America and why we were visiting Tobati. He pointed at Naomi: "You brought this little girl all the way from America?" His face was concerned at first, but then when I nodded, he smiled. "Why did you want to come to Paraguay? We are a very small, very poor nation," he said. I told him that I thought Paraguay had a very interesting history and many beautiful sites. I explained that we had been climbing and exploring the rocky hills and majestic outcroppings that surrounded Tobati, and that we were really enjoying ourselves. I went on to tell him that we also wanted to visit Paraguay to see how God was working among his children. "I believe that God loves all of his creation," I said, "and He is working and healing and calling all people to himself." The man explained that he grew up in the Roman Catholic Church, but that there was a lot of corruption, so he lost interest in his later years. "The important thing for me," I explained, "is to know that God loves us. He loved us enough to send his only Son Jesus Christ to suffer and to die for our sins. By faith in Christ we find forgiveness for our failures, and I have many!" I squeezed the man's shoulder when I told him how much I needed the grace and forgiveness of God, and he laughed with me. When we left the man's home he put his hand on my shoulder, "Thank you," he said, "thank you for coming to Paraguay, and thank you for showing me the love of God."

God's pickaxe had plunged all the way through my reservations, and the tears that shot to my eyes were evidence that my reservations had given way to new hope in making a significant and loving connection. This wasn't about selling an idea or delivering a pitch; this was about sitting and talking and sharing hope. I was not a great white American savior, but just one broken man sharing the hope I'd found in Christ.

The next house we visited was Kendra's friend, the widow. Before we clapped outside her garden, I patted Naomi and Taylor on the shoulders: "You two take the lead on this one. Share your hearts and trust that the Lord will give you the right words." Though clearly uncomfortable with this proposition, they nodded and we clapped. The old woman came out to meet us with a bright smile. She led us through a beautiful garden and into her living room. Shaded by giant trees, her open-style living room was cool and comfortable. She pointed to the couch, and asked us to sit down. She told Kendra that she had some juice she would like to share with us, and rushed out of the room. In just a few moments she returned from the kitchen with a carafe of juice and an assortment of cookies. Before we poured the juice she wanted to lead us on a tour of her house.

Leading us down a hallway off from the living room, she pointed to dozens of pictures hanging on the wall. She told us about her husband and her children. She told us about her own family, and how she moved to Tobati from a very small village in the hills. Kendra smiled and remarked to her that Tobati was a very small village. The woman laughed and said, "As a teenager, the first cars I'd ever seen were here in Tobati. Out in the hills where I grew up, it is only horses and donkeys and lots of animals, a very simple life with very little social interaction."

She showed us each bedroom, explaining who was living in each room now, and expressing gratitude that the house was full of family. When we returned to the living room the woman asked us why we had come to Paraguay. Taylor and I met eyes, and she smiled. She explained the nature of our trip and about our desire to learn about what God was doing all around the world. The woman was shocked that we'd chosen Paraguay for our itinerary, but then she locked eyes on Naomi. At this time Naomi was ten years old and very blonde. The woman began asking her questions, and Naomi answered very clearly. I was really impressed as she told the woman about her faith in God's love, and about the fact that she was excited by all the things she had learned about God in different countries.

Something about Naomi's and Taylor's words made the woman emotional. She told us that she missed her husband, and that she also missed many other dear friends who had died in recent years. She told us that she believed that God loved her, but it was really powerful for her to hear Naomi and Taylor speak about God's grace and kindness. As we left the woman's home, Kendra reminded her that she could come get discounted food at the Su Refugio pantry, if she needed some help. The woman gave us big hugs, patted us each on the shoulders, and smiled as we left her garden.

The Lord did not settle for digging a hole four feet wide and six feet deep into my reservations that day. He skillfully removed the fears and the uncertainties around my heart and mind, and I sensed that he was opening an artesian well of faith in my spirit. This was work I could not accomplish on my own—I could not arrive at this place of faith by relying on my own wit and charm. We broke real bread and entered into a sacred place with strangers by the guidance of Almighty God.

Romania:
"New Friends
and New Vision"

We were packed into a Romanian coffee shop with fifty or more men and women. It was free-lunch Saturday, and the church opened its doors and the services of its kitchen to serve the homeless community of Oradea a free lunch. The aroma of dark-roast coffee blended with the stench of body odor and urine. Pastor Cornel Caba stood with me and told me how this Saturday tradition started. "I'm embarrassed that we waited so long to get this going," he said. Pastor Caba started New Life Church in his home. When the church outgrew his living room, instead of looking for a building, Pastor Caba and the elders purchased a cafe. He continued, "This city has many beautiful churches, but I think many folks are suspicious of the professional clergy here. When they come here they see a coffee shop; they see real life, and they see Jesus worshiped in the middle of it all." Pastor Caba gestured to one of my students who was helping a homeless woman organize her belongings in the corner of the cafe. Adam and I had instructed the team to spread out in the cafe, to avoid taking up the limited seats, and to look for ways to serve and interact in helpful ways. Our students were very skilled at this kind of work, many of them having a wonderful sense of intuition and a genuine interest in meeting and learning from others.

Pastor Caba explained that many Romanians see church as a thing to do on Sunday. He was also concerned that too many believed that religion was for the clergy, not for working professionals and normal people. Even though New Life Church is big enough to pay a pastor full time, Pastor Caba insists that he must keep his regular job in order to be an example to the people in the wider community. As an executive in the travel industry, Pastor Caba felt called into this tent-making style of ministry. He said, "When I tell people outside the church that I have a real job (smirking), I remove an excuse as well as a stumbling block. I work all week, yet still I make time to worship with the church, to involve myself in service to the community, and to pray."

Talking about the free-lunch Saturday tradition, Pastor Caba explained that it started as a one-time New Year's event. At the beginning of every new year, he and his leadership team spend a significant time fasting and praying for a new vision for the year ahead. The leadership felt strongly that God was calling them to start a lunch program on Saturdays. The event was successful right away, and by the end of the first month it was clear that they were to continue this tradition for the year. Pastor Caba said, "Once God had made this vision clear to us, I was a bit embarrassed. We should have started this much sooner. Our Heavenly Father is patient!"

Pastor Caba explained that shortly after the church started serving free lunch on Saturdays, the demographic of the church changed. He said, "Many of the people that came for lunch also started coming to Sunday service. Some of the original members had a problem with this, complaining about the bad smell." Caba's response: "The church is for all of God's children." Many of the homeless men and women also started meeting together for weekly Bible studies in the park. Pastor Caba invited them to become members, and to take responsibility for cleaning and caring for the facility with the entire congregation. He was insistent that there would be no insiders or outsiders—just a church family.

The New Life Church congregation runs its coffee shop with evangelistic aims. One of the baristas is a San Diego native named Sierra, who felt called to move to Oradea after a two-week mission trip with her church three years prior. She said, "I pray as I make drinks, and I look for opportunities to encourage our guests. There are many opportunities to share the Gospel, especially with the regulars."

In addition to the daily operations of the coffee shop, New Life Church hosts weekly Mommy and Me groups in the large cafe garden. Children play in the sandbox or swing on the jungle gym while young mothers sip coffee and enjoy a relaxing conversation. The church also runs a school in Lazareni, a very poor Roma community outside the city.

During our stay in Oradea we joined Pastor Caba's team and helped them with some projects in Lazareni. The Lazareni team was led by a dynamic married couple named Gheorghe and Alina. These two had different responsibilities in this sensitive ministry, and we followed their lead. The ministry among the Roma people is sensitive because of a racial stigma. Some Romanians are distrusting of the Roma people, many of whom seem to float on the edge of the community. Some Roma have been caught stealing and causing other problems in the city, adding to the mistrust. Pastor Caba and his leadership team, though mindful of the challenges, followed Christ's example of loving and serving those whom his society had deemed outcasts or troublemakers. New Life Church began an active campaign to reach out to the Roma people in Oradea as well as in Lazareni.

The drive out to Lazareni took us through some beautiful little Romanian towns. The rolling green hills, white windmills, and winding rocky streams all through the countryside kept me staring out the window. These postcard land-scapes continued along the Crisul River until we reached the turnoff for Lazareni. The quaint homes and tightly organized farmlands gave way to dry hills and a heavily littered roadway. The church purchased a plot of land on the edge of the Roma village. We pulled up to an old barn to the right and left of which stood two small structures. One of the buildings served as a preschool, and the second as an office and thrift store. Gheorghe and Alina walked our team around the property, introducing us to the lead teacher, and describing the projects they planned to have us work on that afternoon.

Five members of our team were needed to move some lumber out of the barn, while several others were asked to help the preschool children with a craft. Several other team members were asked to unload boxes and bags of clothing from the vans, as well as to unpack and sort the clothing and goods in the thrift store. I started in the barn, which was a very rough, very old structure that Gheorghe and other members of the church had recently gutted and secured. Old farm equipment, rusty and broken, as well as several large broken beams lay all around. Gheorghe wanted to preserve these pieces as part of the legacy of the property, but they had to be relocated outside the walking paths and usable areas. He was impressed as some of our young men and women attacked the piles of broken lumber and mangled steel. The barn would one day be an events center for the Roma community, Gheorghe explained. The church hoped to use this property in the same way they used the cafe in town. The preschool, the events center, and the thrift store were not profit-making enterprises, but rather well-organized gathering places that would serve the needs of the families in the neighborhood.

After seeing the work get started in the barn, I walked over to the thrift store. I found our students waist deep in clothing inside the store. The bags of donated clothing had been unpacked, and it seemed there was too much for the tiny room to hold. After two hours the students had organized and folded hundreds of articles of clothing. A women's section, a men's section, and a children's section were created, and although the clothing still seemed to spill out of the room, a customer could easily navigate his way through the options. After two hours Alina poked her head into the store and announced the fact that a line of customers was forming along the sidewalk outside. All articles of clothing in the store were priced at one Romanian leu, equivalent to 25 US cents. Standing in front of the store, Alina shared with me how the store had become very popular. "We noticed that very few people in the village had jackets, and many were wearing old, ripped pants as well as broken shoes," Alina explained. "We used to bring bags of clothes into the village, passing them out to various families. Some of our friends here told us that many of the people were embarrassed to accept free clothing," she said. The idea for the store came from a few of the leaders in the Roma community. The property was falling apart, and the barn and buildings were too old and dangerous to occupy. The community leaders suggested that the church purchase the property and to sell the donated clothing at a discounted rate. After several months of research, the church made a plan to not only offer a store, but added the preschool and the event center. The Roma leadership was thrilled, and it was not long before the school was at capacity and the store a wild success.

After we closed up the thrift shop and locked up the barn, Gheorghe and Alina walked us up into the center of the neighborhood. Homes of broken plywood and sheet metal lined the road through Lazareni. There was an outhouse and a water pump every 50 yards or so, very few of the homes having their own private water or sewage systems. As we walked through the town it seemed that people did not want to interact with us. The doors and windows of the homes we passed were tightly boarded up, and no one came out to greet us. At the far end of the town we found a group of boys playing soccer on a dirt field, and a few of our students walked over to meet them. A new game was organized, and while our students wanted to mix into the present game, the Roma boys apparently wanted to show the Americans how to play. Although we had some good athletes on our team, the Roma boys knew how to navigate the weeds and potholes on the field with great skill. The Roma team was soon off to a commanding lead.

During the game Gheorghe asked me to follow him to a friend's house near the field. He led me across the street to a small structure guarded by a large metal door. The windows were nailed over with a thick metal screen. Gheorghe knocked on the door and called out in Romanian, "Darius! Este Gheorghe." The door cracked open, a chain still attached on the inside, and then some shuffling followed by a loud greeting from inside: "Gheorghe!" A thick-shouldered man ducked through the doorway and crashed into Gheorghe with a bear hug. The two men smiled and patted each other's arms, laughing and sharing some kind words. Gheorghe gestured toward me and said, "This is a friend of our church, John Norton. He brought some students from America. They helped us on the property today." Darius held out a hand. As I shook Darius' hand, Gheorghe put his hand on top of ours and said, "This is my good friend, Darius. He has a beautiful family, a wife and three girls..." His friend interrupted him, "And a new baby boy?" Gheorghe erupted in laughter. Darius called out to his wife, and in a moment she ducked through the door with a tiny baby in her arms. Gheorghe leaned to look at the baby, and the woman pushed the child into Gheorghe's chest. He leaned down and kissed the little boy's forehead: "Ah, what a handsome boy!" He reached over and pulled Darius' wife into a hug and began praying in Romanian. Darius put his hand on Gheorghe's back, and I put one hand on Gheorghe and one hand on Darius.

When Gheorghe finished praying we backed up a step, and Darius and his wife wiped tears from their eyes. Gheorghe told me later that he prayed a blessing on the child, and that he also prayed a blessing on Darius' home. I had been a bit uncomfortable moments earlier as we approached this well-protected home. The metal edges and chain mail that secured the home now faded from view, and I saw something precious and beautiful.

When we drove back to Oradea that evening Erica and I sat beside Gheorghe and Alina. I could see that they were energized by the vision and love God gave them for the Roma village. Gheorghe said, "We are doing something very small, but it feels really good to get involved. I have seen this community of people pushed farther and farther out of the city, and now they seem abandoned in a wasteland." Outside the window we were passing a brightly lit town with beautiful lawns and manicured gardens. From the road I could see open pubs and restaurants, and many people out and interacting. Although we were now a few miles away from Lazareni, Gheorghe seemed to still see the property, Darius and his wife, and their little baby boy. He said, "Many of the Roma people are honest, hard-working folks who want to see their community thrive. The Lazareni neighborhood was once very dark and desperate, but now we are seeing new light there. These are our friends, and we want to join them in their struggles, but also in their hopes for a better future for their children."

Nepal:
"Rescue in Mamling"

"When you use a squatty potty here in Nepal, you have to pull up your skirt, get your balance secure, and drop all the way down." This comical and very practical advice came from our host in Nepal, and it had all of us bent over in laughter. Sandra Baltimore is barely five feet tall, but her personality and her loving, caring attitude makes her seem as big as an NBA superstar. She and her husband Robert met while studying in the States, but Sandra grew up in Argentina and Robert in Ohio. The two started dreaming about mission work before marriage, and after years of praying, they realized God was calling them to Nepal.

The Baltimore's are *first contact* missionaries, meaning that they focus on taking the Gospel to those who have never heard it. In Nepal this means hiking for days, and sometimes weeks, into the Himalayan foothills. In addition to the clothing in their backpacks, the Baltimores carry a projector and a copy of *The Jesus Film*. As an amateur magician, Robert carries several ropes and other fun supplies that allow him to put on informal magic shows. These tricks always draw a crowd of children, but the tricks are also good enough to attract adults too.

Another of the gifts Robert shared with our team was his training as a wilderness emergency medical technician (EMT). His knowledge of the human body and his ability to diagnose a serious medical condition allowed us to get important and timely medical care for one of my students. It all happened quite unexpectedly when we were staying in a remote village in the foothills of the Himalayas.

The Baltimores led our team to Mamling, a village where they had established a church a few years before. This growing body of believers was holding an ordination service for a few new pastors, and the Baltimores made arrangements for our team to join them. The small village of Mamling was located in the foothills of the Himalayan mountains—a 26-hour bus ride northeast of Kathmandu. While this bus ride involved bumpy terrain and tight, winding roads, this was light work for the Baltimores. They were accustomed to walking for several hours each day—our cramped bus was a luxury for them. Our bus ride turned into a four-wheeled adventure when we got within ten miles of the village. The narrow mountain roads were bumpy, and it took a special vehicle and a special set of driving skills to navigate them safely. At various points on the way to Mamling the road provided only enough space for one vehicle, and just as Robert started to explain the problems that often happen when a car breaks down, we pulled up in a long line of traffic.

Robert jumped off the bus and waved for me to follow him. We walked along the side of a deeply grooved dirt road with a very steep cliff on the far side. The grooves in the road were at least three to four feet deep in certain sections, completely impassable without four-wheel drive and significant ground clearance. We walked for about two hundred yards when we saw the problem. A jeep was stuck in one of the deep grooves, and its front axle had snapped. Robert talked to a few of the men surrounding the vehicle and gathered that while help was on the way, the road would be blocked for several hours.

While Robert walked ahead to negotiate with some of the Nepali bus drivers on the other side of the accident, I walked back to the team. Adam and I had the students gather on the side of the road, sitting on rocks and tree stumps, and we held class. On a curve that overlooked some of the most beautiful mountains in the world, we discussed Nepali literature and culture.

Robert returned an hour later. He had walked to the other side of the accident and found a bus like ours. He arranged for the drivers to trade vehicles and we were on our way. I remember marveling at the ease with which Robert made these kinds of negotiations. God gifted him with a personality that gained him a lot of favor with the Nepali people. It was amazing to see someone whom the Lord had so clearly prepared for this work. He and Sandra continued to inspire us, but as we would soon discover, the real challenges had not even begun.

In addition to filling out the seats at the ordination service, our team designed and led an English camp for the village school. It was a small K-12 school, and the principal was thrilled to have a team of Americans teaching his students English for a week. He had no problem with our use of Bible stories in the camp, and we ended up using a Vacation Bible School structure to teach the students English.

Our accommodations in Mamling were particularly memorable. The women stayed in the church sanctuary and the men broke up into small groups and stayed in church member's homes. My family stayed in a barn that had been outfitted with four plywood beds. On our second night, I discovered that my nightstand was actually a large bucket of goat food with a piece of plywood on top. Despite the company of mice that scampered in and out of our little house, the room was warm and cozy. Thick hand-woven blankets provided plenty of cushion on our plank beds, and our hosts provided a pot of hot water for coffee and fresh-squeezed goat milk for us each morning at daybreak. I'll never forget stepping out of the barn after our first night in Mamling. I had to duck out of our doorway, and when I straightened up I was face-to-face with Mount Makalu, the fifth-highest mountain in the world. As the crow flies, we were approximately 70 miles from Mount Makalu. Because of its immense size, stretching over 27,000 feet into the sky, it seemed like it was right on top of us. It is hard to describe what a mountain like this can do to the human spirit. I found myself in prayer each morning, wanting to sing to the Lord and to praise his glory.

Our English camp was packed with kids. At certain points during that week I had to fill in at various stations just to help keep control over the massive group of campers. We told Bible stories, shared about Christ and his resurrection, taught about American culture, and played fun games. The team was in high spirits, and I think we all knew that this experience and these memories would stay with us forever. When a few of us developed stomach issues—diarrhea is a common challenge for travelers—I was not worried. From teat-fresh milk to nest-fresh eggs, I assumed that our bodies would undergo some shock. It was when I saw Taylor Doornbos doubled over in tears in my Nepali literature class that I grew concerned.

Taylor was a fantastic traveler—tough, enthusiastic, adventurous. She was really close to my daughter Naomi, and we all respected her ability to handle anything. Knowing that Robert was an EMT with a lot of medical experience, I planned to ask him to take a look at her. Before I brought it up he had spotted the worrying signs. "I'm concerned about Taylor's appendix," he told me after class. After asking her about the pain, Robert was confident that we needed to get Taylor down the mountain and to a hospital as soon as possible. He snapped into action by arranging for a taxi and fashioning a stretcher out of some long bamboo poles and a large tarp. We carried Taylor down to the main road and sent her with Professor Lee and Joanna Steinhaus to the hospital in Bijaipur.

It turned out that although Taylor's appendix had ruptured, her body formed a wall around it. The doctor in Kathmandu communicated with Taylor's doctor at home in the States and determined that the appendectomy could be safely postponed to the end of the semester. Taylor was adamant about staying on the trip. She was determined to finish the semester, to stay with the team, and to experience the full ATW semester.

This event in Nepal will forever be a testimony of God's goodness and faithfulness to me. From Robert and Sandra's insight and care for our team, and especially their ability to read Taylor and her needs, to God's miraculous protection of Taylor by walling off her appendix. These events are a beautiful and very personal reminder of God's continued grace and care.

India:
"Air Conditioning
and Friendship"

Famed travel writer, Pico Ayer, describes India and its massive scale as "an inflation of humanity and an intensification of humanity." We were unprepared for this kind of intensity on our first trip to India in 2010. Although we learned powerful lessons about God's grace and generosity through a Lutheran church community in Mumbai, the weather, the food, and the culture of India over-whelmed us. Four years later, when we announced a return trip to India, my kids were upset. In a moment of inspiration, I asked them what kinds of things would make India enjoyable. Without a pause, Jack said, "air conditioning" and laughed as if it was an impossibility. Naomi was quiet for a moment, and then said, "A friend." I told them these things were not impossible, and that I would do whatever I could to make this next trip to India a bit more comfortable for them. I could not promise friends or citywide air conditioning, but we would pray and ask God to help us plan a good trip. For the next year, as we planned and prepared to launch the trip, we prayed through the itinerary. Every time we prayed about India, the kids asked God for good air conditioning and good friendships.

We landed in Kolkata in early October of 2014. The bus dropped us off in front of a large apartment building, and we met our hosts on the fourth floor. The accommodations were very simple, but everyone had a bed. While the students were assigned rooms, our host pulled me aside with a concerned look on his face. "We do not have room for the professors and your family in this building; we will be sending you to a hotel down the street," he said. As we slipped under our backpacks and followed him outside, I whispered the news to

Erica and we braced for the worse. As we walked on the sidewalk along AJC Bose Road, I prayed. I had a soul-changing experience in Kolkata two years before while serving at the Mother Teresa Homes. God worked a miracle in my spirit on that trip, and I felt a deep fondness for this city. I wanted my family to share my love for the Mother Teresa Homes and for this amazing city. The noise of honking horns and dense traffic made it impossible to talk as we walked, but I could see that the kids were uncomfortable and nervous.

Our host led us to Hotel Heaven, which was the closest building to the Mother Teresa home. This was a good sign, and as we stepped into the lobby we experienced a second good sign—crisp, cool air conditioning. Jack looked up at me right away, "Dad, do you think our room will be this cold?" I smiled and said, "I don't know buddy, but I hope so." We made plans to meet our host back at the apartment building in a couple of hours, and the bellhop showed us to our room.

It was a spacious room with two large beds and a pullout couch. The air conditioning was pumping, and the room felt like the inside of a freezer. Jack dropped his backpack with a dramatic flair and fell backward onto one of the beds. He laughed and said, "Yes! I love this place!" Prayer number one: answered. I reminded Jack of this prayer, and he nodded and said, "Can we just spend 14 days in this room, dad?" I explained how much fun we would have working together at the Mother Homes, and that before they started worrying about discomfort, to remember that God was already starting to answer prayers.

Service with Mother Teresa's Missionaries of Charity always begins at 6:00am at the Mother Home. After a traditional Roman Catholic worship service on the second floor of the home, the volunteers are invited to gather in a big workroom on the ground floor where a simple breakfast is served: bananas, sliced white bread, and hot chai tea in plastic yellow cups. The sisters lead the volunteers, usually between 20 and 120 adults from all over the world, in a time of prayer and worship as well as through a brief orientation. The sisters do not know who is coming to volunteer each day, and they do not ask anyone to sign up. They trust that God will bring the volunteers needed to serve His children.

While I have never seen the sisters anxious, each time I bring a team of volunteers, I notice a distinct expression of relief on the sisters' faces. When we arrived in 2014, Sister Mercy Maria gave us an approving smile and said, "I am very glad to see you and this big team of strong hands and smiling faces. We have been low on volunteers lately, and your team will give each of the homes a nice boost." There are few things I am more proud to receive than an approving smile from Sister Mercy Maria. She is not a very talkative person, but when she does speak, she does so with intention and purpose. She reached down and patted our two-year-old Sheffield on the head; he was standing beside me. "Now this little guy will not be going with you to the homes, right? He is too young yet," she said. I nodded and told her that Erica and I would be taking turns going to Daya Dan with Jack and Naomi. One of us would have a separate adventure in Kolkata with Sheffield every other day.

Our team was broken into five different groups, with each small group heading to a different home: Daya Dan, Prem Dan, Shanti Dan, Kalighat, and Shishu Bavan. Each home has a different kind of resident population: some homes care for people with special needs, others for men and women recovering from addiction, and others for those near death. Because Jack and Naomi were young, the sisters asked our family to serve at Daya Dan, a home for children with disabilities.

Traveling from the Mother Home to the various ministry homes is always tricky and often hectic, as the traffic in Kolkata is world famous. The sisters have a wonderful system in place, and before they dismiss the different groups to leave for the homes, they ask someone who has been serving for a while to be the leader. The sisters also ask these groups to travel together, always warning the volunteers to be careful in crowds, and to avoid walking alone. "Like in any big city," Sister Mercy Maria explains each morning, "there are wonderful people here in Kolkata, but there are also desperate people who are willing to do desperate things. When you stick together, you are less likely to be taken advantage of by a desperate person."

This was their first time visiting Daya Dan, so Erica and the kids followed a group of volunteers who knew the way. The morning trek took 30 minutes, and it required that they walk about a half mile, jump on a tightly packed bus for three miles, and then flag down a rickshaw for the final mile. Because the Mother Homes attract thousands of volunteers each year, the local bus drivers and rickshaw drivers are usually helpful. Erica and I explained to the kids how important it was to pay attention, as the driving patterns in Kolkata are very organic, and cars may even slip up onto a sidewalk if it allows them to avoid an accident or a slower driver. Erica held Naomi's hand tightly on these trips through the intense traffic and the horn-honking madness, but Naomi never looked concerned. Jack was now a tall, muscular boy, and he had successfully transitioned into Erica's protector. This new role did not suit Erica, as she still wanted to coddle Jack a bit, but he was very serious about keeping any desperate-looking men away from his mom.

Later that first week, on a different bus ride through the city, I saw a man on the bus put his hand on a railing that was suspiciously close to Erica's rear end. Just as I was about to step in to intercept, Jack slid between the man and Erica. Although Jack was smiling, he made it very clear that the man needed to move his hand away from Erica. I was so proud of my protective boy at that moment, his thoughtful eyes aware of the surroundings.

When our team arrived at Daya Dan each day, the house helpers, called *mashis*, greeted us and sent us to the roof to help with laundry. The entire washing facility was located on the roof, and it consisted of three giant, square, concrete sinks, a long empty table, and 25 rows of wire laundry lines. Two sinks were filled with soapy water and a third with fresh water. The sisters appointed a volunteer to manage each sink. The person in front of the soapy sink would dip and squeeze different articles of clothing. After dipping and kneading a shirt, for instance, the worker would then pass that shirt to the worker on his left. That worker would follow the same process, and then pass the shirt to the final sink, which was full of fresh rinsing water. This worker would rinse the shirt and then lay it on the long table to his left where three more workers waited for final wringing. When a large bucket was filled with washed clothing, it was picked up by another set of workers who shook out the clothing and hung it on a series of laundry lines that covered most of the roof. The laundry takes about an hour to complete, depending on volume and on how many volunteers are working. When the laundry is complete, the mashis on the roof point to the stairs and say, "Finish. Go!"

Many of my students were shocked at first with how brusquely they are treated by the mashis. The combination of an intense workload and limited

English comprehension is what often results in a harsh tone. I have had great success bonding with the mashis, because I go out of my way to joke with them, compliment them, and care for them. I push past what seems a harsh or angry tone and pour on the smiles with a funny but respectful snapping to attention. I warned Erica and the kids about this, and in their own ways, they ended up connecting with many of these hard-working helpers.

On their first day of service, Erica and the kids came down the laundry stairs not knowing what to expect. The main floor of the children's home is painted in bright colors and an open skylight allows lots of fresh, natural light into the main living room. The children sit in different spots all around this big open room, some in wheelchairs, some in high chairs, and some in beanbags on the floor. Some of the able-bodied children walk around freely, engaging volunteers or playing with toys. Erica, Jack, and Naomi spread out among the children on the floor, looking for ways to play, to connect, or to serve. Naomi found a little two-year-old girl on the floor next to one of the beanbags. "She was the cutest little girl," Naomi told me later, "but she could not walk." When the mashis saw Naomi and Puja connecting, they encouraged Naomi to help her stand and walk along the railing that circled the room. This became Naomi's ritual with Puja each day, participating in all of her therapies and exercises. Because of Naomi's experience in caring for two-year-old Sheffield, she had confidence with Puja, picking her up, squeezing her, and making her laugh.

On her third day at Daya Dan, while still caring for Puja, Naomi was given a glimpse at the darker side of humanity. When she was asked to change Puja's clothes, messy after eating lunch, Naomi saw something she would never forget. "On her tiny little back there were deep, red scars," Naomi said, "it looked like someone had beaten her with something very sharp that tore her skin." There were also burn marks on Puja's back. All of this was very confusing to Naomi, and I will never forget trying to answer her primary question—what kind of evil person would strike and torture a baby? This was a hard discussion, but I talked with her about sin and the desperation that exists in all men and women. Sin can lead people to do horrific things. Our hope is in Christ's death and resurrection, which results in our forgiveness. The hope we have in Christ is greater than all the sin in the world, I explained to Naomi. Christ's love and hope inspires and instructs people like Mother Teresa. Our Heavenly Father not only forgives sins, but His Holy Spirit fills the redeemed with holy passion—passion that leads to the rescue and care of these precious children. It was in those holy moments of caring for Puja that God inspired Naomi to want to become a nurse. At 10 years of age, and in that very special home, Naomi was powerfully moved by God's love for the suffering. She wanted to be part of the healing and part of the cure.

After our first week of service, Naomi managed to tell everyone on our ATW team about her sweet friend Puja. Every day Naomi had a new story about something she was able to help Puja accomplish or about a game they played together. One of Naomi's most memorable days was when the mashis asked her to help them fit glasses on Puja's face. They were a special type that wrapped around her ears, and at first, she refused to wear them. When Naomi showed Puja how she put on her own glasses, the problem was solved—Puja seemed content to wear glasses like her friend Naomi.

It took us until the middle of our second week to realize that Puja was the answer to Naomi's prayer for a friend in India. When I mentioned this to Naomi, her eyes lit up. I saw faith growing in my little daughter's heart, and I was overcome with a powerful gratitude for our Savior's faithful care.

Cambodia: "Returning to the Site of the Murder"

On January 7, 1979, Vietnamese troops stormed into Phnom Penh, the capital city of Cambodia. While the brutal dictator Pol Pot was overthrown, the carnage he orchestrated as leader decimated nearly one third of the Cambodian population. After the war Pol Pot retreated into the jungle, and for many years he and his Khmer Rouge party continued to taunt the Cambodian government with guerilla actions.

In the fall of 2014, we traveled to Cambodia to work with the Hope Bible Institute. Our Cambodian host Sambath met us outside of our hotel in Phnom Penh. He gave us a short introduction to the ministry, and promised that we would hear more about it after our five-hour drive northwest to a city called Battambang. We loaded our bags into a white minivan and a red, open-sided truck, outfitted with benches and a metal roof. Although the temperature and the humidity soared above 90°F, the drive was beautiful, especially once we got outside of the capital city. The Cambodian rural communities are carved into lush green jungles, bursting with color and life.

When we arrived at the ten-acre campus of the Hope Bible Institute, Sambath introduced us to the campus pastor and his wife. This dynamic couple organized all of our meals, and helped Sambath arrange a series of ministry projects we would participate in for two weeks. The campus was very pretty, with a big green lawn surrounded by a horseshoe-shaped, single-story building which included dorms, classrooms, and the main office. There were two additional buildings: the kitchen and the church.

During our stay, the testimonies of God's faithfulness to this community of Cambodian Christians inspired and humbled our team. One of our hosts told us his story of escaping Pol Pot's genocidal terror in the 1970s. His father was a doctor and cared for the Khmer Rouge military. Suspicion and paranoia haunted every corner of society, and these two toxic partners had an especially strong hold on the military ranks. Many of his friends had been mysteriously disappearing, and rumors of secret murders were circling. Late one night his father returned home and ordered everyone to follow him into the jungle. They ran for many hours, all through the night, finally arriving at the Thai border. Along the way, he described having to step over hundreds of dead bodies left to rot in the jungle.

Another of our hosts was a teenager when Pol Pot and his terrifying Khmer Rouge came to power. Although he was only 15, the government conscripted him into the army, and forced him to dig graves and carry equipment. One night his commander ordered him to appear before a panel of officers. The commander led him and three others 100 yards from their encampment in the jungle. He knew he was going to be shot. The commander ordered the four boys to drop to their knees. He cocked his revolver and asked them each to bow their heads. When our host bowed his head, his cross necklace slipped out from behind his shirt. The cross had been a gift from his mother, and although he was not a Christian, he promised his mother to always wear it. When the commander stepped in front of our host to shoot him, the officer saw the cross and poked it with his finger. At that moment the officer and his helpers were suddenly called away to take care of a different matter. When the officers were out of sight, our host said that he and his three friends took off running. They ran all night. After several hours they crossed the Thai border. He said that for the next two years he moved from refugee camp to refugee camp. In one camp, he heard a man talking about the Gospel. He told this man about his experience with the commander, the cross, and his escape. The man told him about the grace and love of God, and he led our host to Christ.

Over our two-week stay, we heard many more stories about the horrific devastation of Pol Pot's reign of terror. We also heard many stories of redemption and grace, the most powerful part involving God's call on many refugees to return to Cambodia. Many of these men and women lost parents and siblings, relatives, and many close friends to the genocidal Khmer Rouge. In spite of all this, God planted forgiveness in their hearts, and each felt His call to return to Cambodia. Tragically, although Pol Pot was removed from leadership, few of the Khmer Rouge were ever brought to justice. The men and women who served as our hosts in Cambodia explained that God called them back to Cambodia to minister to the very people who murdered their loved ones.

God placed a man named Christopher LaPel at the helm of the Hope Bible Institute. Christopher's story of loss and redemption is also dramatic. After the Khmer Rouge murdered his parents and siblings, Christopher fled to Thailand where he became a Christian in a refugee camp. He met his wife in one of these camps, and from there God called him into ministry in Southern California. Christopher became a pastor and opened a church in Long Beach, where he ministers to many Cambodian immigrants and refugees—men and women who suffered just as he had. After serving in Long Beach for three years, Christopher felt God's call to begin making trips back to Cambodia and many others began to follow. On one of his trips, Christopher was preaching and baptizing new Christians in the jungles outside of Battambang. At the conclusion of one of these sessions, a man approached. "Pastor," he said, "if a man has killed someone, can he still receive the forgiveness of God?" Christopher said yes. "Ok, pastor, if a man has killed ten people, can he still receive the forgiveness of God?" Christopher replied yes, again. The man broke down in tears: "Pastor, if a man has killed hundreds and hundreds of people, can he receive the forgiveness of God?" At this moment, Pastor Christopher knew he was speaking with a member of the Khmer Rouge party. What he did not know was that this man was the notorious leader of the S-21 prison, who presided over the brutal torture and murder of more than 14,000 innocent men, women, and children.

After leading this man to Christ, Pastor Christopher found out that his name was Kaing Guek Eav, better known by his Khmer Rouge name, Duch. Duch was the fourth highest-ranking officer in the Khmer Rouge regime. After his conversion, Duch turned himself in to the government authorities, and he was given a life sentence in prison. Christopher and many of his team members forgave Duch over time. Duch was an active Christian believer, sharing the hope of the Gospel with many, until his death in prison in 2020.

Sambath and his ministry partners invited us to follow them into the jungles outside of Battambang where many of the leaders of the Khmer Rouge were still living. These criminals fled to the jungles to escape the new Cambodian government established after Pol Pot was overthrown. Although we never met Pastor Christopher, it was a great honor to experience his ministry influence and to visit several of the small village churches he planted. My team of students performed Bible stories for the children and talked with the adults. We did not speak about the atrocities of war, but of the war for our souls. We did not preach about the evil of genocide, but rather about the peace offered to all people through Christ and about the love He promises to put into the hearts of all believers.

During our stay in Cambodia, we visited the S-21 prison as well as The Killing Fields Memorial Park. It was painful to walk these grounds with Jack and Naomi, who were very aware of the horrors committed at each site. We talked about sin and hatred, prejudice and power. We also talked about the incredible presence of God in Cambodia—something we all felt in a palpable way.

The Hope Bible campus pastor asked me to preach to the church on our final Sunday in Battambang. As I walked up to the podium I started to sweat, my hands shaking. I felt poorly equipped to teach such a powerful group of heroic Christian believers. I looked out at 50 men and women who had suffered some of the worst government atrocities in human history. These men and women did not dissolve into self-pity, nor did they explode with rage and revenge. Each had been rescued by the love and grace of God through faith in Christ Jesus. Each had been transformed, now able to forgive the horrific crimes committed against their families and friends. These men and women forgave their Khmer Rouge brothers "seven times seventy" as Jesus instructs in the Gospels, and miraculously they responded to God's call to return to the site of the murder with the good news of the Gospel.

PART 4

ATW 2016

When the 2014 ATW team returned to campus, they added to the growing excitement behind the ATW program. Adam and I felt that it was time to expand the program, allowing more students to join the adventure. We planned to offer ATW every fall, beginning with the fall semester of 2016. Adam would lead a team in the fall of 2016, and I would stay back to design, prepare, and lead a trip in the fall of 2017.

Adam would lead the 2016 trip with our good friends Tony and Heather Vezner. Tony was a theater professor and Heather an education professor at Concordia. They were a fantastic addition to our leadership team, and much like Tim and Debbie Preuss, I knew the Vezners would bring some wonderful insights to the program.

Although it was exciting to see our program growing and expanding to an every-year model, I felt the same mixed emotions for the 2016 team as I felt for the 2012 team. This group of students was very strong and dynamic, and I was sorry to miss the opportunity to work with them—as well as with Adam, Tony, and Heather.

Preparations for the fourth ATW Semester began in January of 2015.

Leadership Team:

Adam Lee	Tony and Heather Vezner*
Sam Bretzmann (GA)	Alanna Bretzmann (GA)
Ryan Fink (GA)	Jessica Schrank (GA)

*The Vezner children: Olivia (18) and Ben (16)

Student Team:

Anthony Draper	Christian Woodfin
Adam Dougherty	Dale Allison
William Bakker	Kaitlyn Bird
Claire Brainard	McKenna Brand
Jordan Dakin	Brittany Edwards
Alice Fackler	Samuel Fluegge
Joshua Foss	Madison Haase
Michael Hammerle	Kimberly Harding
Kyleigh Hoye	Rachel Kim
Lindsay Lake	Maile Lane
Nyssa McCarthy	Laura Mietzner
Anastasia Rosnau	Brianna Silva
Kendra Sitton	Jonathan Stueve
Lauren Tom	Ryan Van Dusen
Olivia Vezner	Vinh Vu

Itinerary

Japan—China—India—Greece—Czech—England—Ghana—Morocco—
Ecuador—Costa Rica

PART 5

ATW 2017

The 2016 program ended with some exciting news—the announcement that Adam was engaged to be married. He and his fiancé Annett were not only being called into matrimony but also onto the mission field. In the spring of 2017 Adam and Annett moved to Germany to begin their new life together.

While this news made me very happy for Adam, I was losing my ATW partner. Planning, leading, and traveling with Adam was like traveling with family—he was a brother to Erica and me, and he was like an uncle to our kids. I needed to build a new support team, but I knew that no one could replace Adam. His cultural insights were legendary, and he had a profound ability to make connections between literature, life, and the Christian faith.

Tony, Heather, and the 2016 student team returned to campus with some great energy, and they were a huge help to me in my efforts to launch the 2017 team. Another boost to the planning and launching of the 2017 program was the hiring of Alex Lange. Alex and his fiancé Anne took giant leaps of faith to join our leadership team. Sensing God's call on their lives, they moved up their wedding date and quit their full-time jobs to lead the trip with Erica and me. In the early months of trip planning, Erica and I recognized that Alex and Anne were not only an amazing gift to the program but also a wonderful gift to our family.

Preparations for the fifth ATW Semester began in January of 2016.

Leadership Team:

John and Erica Norton*	Alex and Anne Lange
Noah Menke	Taylor Quijada

*The Norton children: Jack (15), Naomi (13), Sheffield (4)

Student Team:

Trevor O'Reilly	Amelia Arnold
Darby Gore	Rachel Finney
Sarah Thompson	Linaya Kolke
Jill May	Maia Jorgensen
Lynnea Marlatt	Kyra Lecakes
Ben Oesch	Liz Balzanti
Youssef Nakhla	Natalia Materazzo
Zachary Winkler	Rachel Moeller
Abigail Vroegindewey	Lauren Kelley
Zane Miller	Abigail DeAllen

Itinerary:

China—Thailand—India—Rwanda—Greece—Germany—Spain—Costa Rica—Guatemala

Tianjin, China: "Playing Catch with Zander"

Zander was sitting by himself in a room full of giggling and gurgling infants. He was holding a small red Matchbox car. I sat on the floor beside him and pointed to the car. He shook his head, shifted his body, and turned his back to me. I slid around his left side and edged closer. He shook his head and covered the car with his other hand when I gestured for him to roll it to me. There were many cars and toys in a blue basket on the far side of the room. I found a similar sized car in the basket and returned to sit beside him. I sat close to him and started driving the car back and forth, revving the engine, and making the car bounce softly off Zander's knee. His eyes bounced from my face to the car I was pushing. When I signaled a desire to roll him my car, he nodded. He tucked his own car securely under his leg and held out his hands. We pushed the car back and forth several times, sometimes spinning it or pretending it was jumping over another toy. We played in this way for 15 minutes until a little blue ball bounced into my lap from across the room. I smiled and held it up; Zander raised his hands. Not knowing if he could catch and not wanting to scare him, I bounced the ball softly toward his lap. Zander not only caught the ball, but he snatched it out of the air with a cocky snap of the wrist. His sudden display of coordination was impressive. He recognized my interest in his skill and smiled. We began a game of catch, slowly moving farther back. We got far enough apart that one of the house mothers shouted at us to take our game outside. On our way out she smiled at me and said, "Zander doesn't speak, at all."

Our host at the Mariner's Harbor Children's Village was a man named Tim Butler. Tim and his wife Pam operated this wonderful home for children with special needs. The home sits on a 15-acre compound in the sleepy outskirts of Tianjin. When we arrived at the facility we were impressed by its beauty. Several gray and white stone buildings with traditional Chinese red, curved-tile roofs graced this compound, and a large, green, grassy lawn stretched out between the buildings. This grassy center area created a park-like setting with big shade trees and a jungle gym area for children.

Our work at Mariner's Harbor involved construction and landscape projects, but also projects involving the children. After a few hours of manual labor each day, our team spread out among the five different children's dorms to play with babies, help with cleaning, or take the bigger kids to the park. On our first day in the homes I sat with a few of the college kids in the middle of a group of eight small children, ages ranging from sixth months to four years old. We tickled them and made them roll over with giggles. In the corner of the room I noticed an older boy sitting by himself. Tim Butler had explained that each of the homes on the compound was organized in a family style structure. Instead of housing all of the infants together in one home, the kids were placed in homes of mixed ages, modeling a real home environment. This is where I had met Zander.

After being kicked out of the home for throwing the ball too aggressively, Zander and I walked to the jungle gym area and found a place to play catch. We made up a few different games, some involving bouncing the ball and some involving rolling it. We had only been playing for about ten minutes when our game was interrupted by one of the Mariner's Harbor therapists. She was a tall American woman in her twenties. She smiled at me and introduced herself as Layel, explaining that it was time for Zander's physical therapy. When she saw that Zander did not want to stop playing, she invited me to join them. I grabbed Zander's hand and we followed Layel to the gym. I participated in Zander's workout, doing his exercises with him, all the while making silly jokes. Layel had a great sense of humor, and she played along.

During the workout Layel explained that Zander was 15 years old and that he had a form of autism that hindered some of his cognitive functioning and particularly his speech. He now understood quite a bit of English and Chinese, and he had grown and developed significantly in his first year of therapy. When he first arrived at Mariner's Harbor, she explained, Zander could do very little for himself. After about a year of therapy, he was now functioning at the cognitive level of a five-year-old, but still no speech. Zander was very coordinated, she explained, and he loved playing catch. "He also loves pulling weeds," Layel said, and with that, the workout was over.

Zander took my hand, understanding before I did that it was time to resume playing in the yard. The mention of weeds must have excited him, because he took me to a spot under a tree in the playground that was overgrown with weeds. His method of weed pulling surprised me, and once again I burst out laughing. He reached down, grabbed the base of the weed, and then threw the weed violently over his shoulder. Dirt from the roots flew everywhere, but Zander didn't mind. He moved quickly across this section of the yard, weeds flying over his shoulder all the while. I followed close enough to be hit by a few flying weeds and tried to keep up with his pace.

I found Zander in his home every afternoon, ready with a ball, and ready to follow me out to the playground. For two weeks we followed this schedule: tossing the ball, working out with Layel, and weeding in the yard. Every now and again Zander wanted to take a weed-pulling break and to swing on the swing set. He never spoke a word, but every day he seemed to smile a bit more frequently, and he even let out a few chuckles. I could tell that he enjoyed my goofy jokes, and he played along with the silly games I proposed. On our last day at Mariner's Harbor, especially as Zander and I were finishing up our weed-pulling time, I started to feel some heavy emotions welling up inside me. This boy had worked his way into my heart, and I really loved his sweet company.

I realized later that it may have been Zander's inability to speak that motivated him to want to play catch. Conversation—really good conversation—is like a game of catch. One partner tosses out an idea, and the other partner catches it and throws it back. Like a great conversation, a game of catch involves creative ways of throwing and catching ideas. A well-matched pair will delight in each other's creative expressions, sometimes impressing and sometimes surprising his partner with something unexpected.

Zander didn't speak one word to me during our two weeks together, but through a creative and extended game of catch, he offered me his friendship.

Thailand: "Banjos and Buddhists"

With a strum of his banjo, Pastor Niran opened up our worship night with the following chorus:

> God is good, all the time,
> He put a song of praise in this heart of mine,
> God is good, all the time,
> Through the darkest night,
> His light will shine, God is good,
> God is good, all the time.

We were packed tight on the roof of our youth hostel in Chiang Mai, a beautiful city in northern Thailand. Pastor Niran and his wife Esther were our hosts, and their personal story of faith and ministry deeply inspired my family and our team of 25 college students. Niran and Esther invited us to serve with them in one of the largest Buddhist elementary schools in the city. The school hired Niran and Esther to teach English and to put on an American culture camp for the entire school. The administration allowed Niran and Esther to use the Bible as an English text, and they were free to talk about their lives, their international travels, and their Christian faith.

Although he was reserved in personal conversation, when he was called upon to lead a group or teach in church Niran was very dynamic. When he introduced our team of students to the 250 kids gathered for our English camp, Niran had their complete attention. With a mix of jokes, questions, and the strum of his banjo, Niran kept the energetic crowd of children transfixed. There was a deep desire in Niran to reach his city for Christ. He knew what it was like to live without hope, trapped in the dark perfectionism of Buddhism.

Not unfamiliar with dark nights, Pastor Niran grew up in a Buddhist home, and in his late teens he moved into the Buddhist temple above Chaing Mai called Wat Phra That Doi Suthep. At this temple Pastor Niran served as a Buddhist monk, meditating and learning the ways of self denial on the *Eightfold Path*. Niran describes his time at the temple with desperate language, confessing that he and his fellow monks were often very depressed, often drawn into substance abuse, and wracked with hopelessness.

During our second week in Chiang Mai, Niran and Esther led us to the Doi Suthep Temple. I walked beside Niran, and he talked about his life as a monk. He said, "There was no real hope here, only the dream of a perfect life that we knew we could not achieve." Doi Suthep was built at the end of the 14th century by King Ku Na. The legend claims that a Buddha relic was placed on the back of a sacred white elephant. The elephant was permitted to roam freely, and it was understood that the elephant would indicate where a new temple should be built. The elephant climbed the Suthep Mountain, trumpeted three times, and walked in three circles. After this dramatic moment the elephant lay down and died. It was understood that the spot where he died would be the location of the new temple, the Wat Phra That Doi Suthep.

Niran explained that during the 1990s the temple was renovated, and the local government invested millions of dollars into its beautification. The central dome in the temple, once a brown stone, was covered in brilliant gold leaf. Several of the other buildings were accented with gold leaf, emphasizing the wealth, status, and success offered to those who dedicated themselves to Buddhism and to the temple's ministry.

Niran said, "I never considered any other options as a young man. Buddhism was all I knew; it was all any of us knew. Until one day, my sister announced that she was getting married. This shocked all of us, because she defied the culture and our religion." Niran's sister announced that she was going to marry a Christian man. Surprisingly, Niran's parents did not disown their daughter for this act, but instead welcomed their new son-in-law into the family. When Niran began to spend time with his new Christian brother-in-law, hearing the Gospel for the first time, his life began to change. The words of hope and grace, real love and the opportunity to be forgiven and cleansed from the stain of sin, changed Niran's heart. The words of the Christian scriptures answered many of his questions about the meaning of life and about his place in the world. He responded to God's love and became a Christian.

When Niran left the monastery, he found a way to attend a Christian seminary, where he met Esther and where the two studied for their divinity degrees. Niran became a pastor in the Lutheran church and Esther became a teacher. Niran now helps train pastors and plant churches from Chiang Mai all the way down to the southern tip of the Thai peninsula. With a banjo slung over his shoulder, Pastor Niran brings hope to those who are trapped in the hopeless perfectionism of the Buddhist faith.

Just as Niran used his banjo to invite my team into worship, he and Esther used their influence in Chiang Mai to invite us into their ministry. We were honored to walk with this generous couple through a city where God is working with miraculous love and power.

Rwanda: "Dirty Sandals, Clean Hearts"

Antoine and Moise met us at the Kigali airport. As they helped load our backpacks onto their bus, they struck up conversations with various members of my college team, and they were quick to offer assistance to those who were not feeling well. When we arrived at the Youth with a Mission (YWAM) base, just outside the city in a town called Rubirizi, these two leaders helped us find our rooms, gave us a campus tour, and briefed us on the history and vision of YWAM Rwanda. Once the team was settled, Antoine and Moise invited our leadership team to sit down for a review of the 14-day schedule they created for us.

It was clear that these two had put some significant time into developing a plan for our team. The schedule fit our academic and study needs perfectly, leaving plenty of time for service learning and adventure in the local area. We were slated to meet with some influential local leaders, women and men whom God raised up to serve and lead in different parts of the local community. These were thoughtful projects, and I was excited to see our team in action.

One of our service-learning opportunities in Rwanda involved work at a school for children with special needs. When Antoine and Moise described the school to our team, it was clear that they held deep respect for the pastor and leader of the organization. When we arrived, we sat down with this pastor, Aloys Ndayizeye, and his story struck us in profound ways. Pastor Ndayizeye was an amazing visionary—his care for the children, and his goal of providing them with an education was not initially accepted by the surrounding community. Many people in the rural areas believed that children with special needs were not capable of learning, and they were seen as a black mark or a curse on their families. Some of these children were given away, but more were just left alone in back rooms. He began a movement in his community, and it was not long before he began to change minds. Each year children are brought to his school from all around Kigali to receive a highly skilled level of instruction in both academic subjects and in personal care. These kids are growing and developing in beautiful ways under the care of Pastor Ndayizeye and his team. After our discussion with Pastor Ndayizeye, our team of 30 split up into four different groups to play games, lead songs, and share stories in different classrooms. The children connected enthusiastically with our team, and we had a lot of fun together.

On one of our days serving at Pastor Ndayizeye's school, he invited Erica and me to sit with a group of single mothers. These were mothers of some of the children in the school, and he told us that their struggles were not uncommon in the community. He asked the women to share their stories with us and he asked us to pray for them. The women told us about the difficulties of raising a child with severe disabilities in a community that sees these children as a curse. Each of the mothers explained the difficulty of finding child care, as many folks in the community did not want their own children to interact with a child with special needs. The mothers shared about their descent into poverty, due to these harmful stigmas, and some felt forced to work in prostitution at times in order to provide for their families.

One mother told us that her financial hardships and the exclusion she felt from the community made her begin to consider suicide. She could see no way out of her predicament. It was that very day that she met one of the mothers from Pastor Ndayizeye's school. She brought her little boy to the school, and right away he and his team began giving her support. Through heavy sobs she explained that for many years she believed her little boy had ruined her life. As she gestured to the friends who now sat around her, and as she spoke about her new faith in Christ, she believed that her son had saved her.

The heat in the church building that morning was stifling, but we were so deeply engrossed in the stories of the women that we had no sense of time passing. When Antoine put his hand on my shoulder, I saw that his eyes were full of tears too. He wanted me to know that the team had finished their program, and that it was time to leave. I couldn't believe we'd been there for over two hours and there was so much I still wanted to say to the women. I stuttered a few words of gratitude for their kindness, for their inspiration, and for their courage. I don't think I was able to say anything more than "thank you," and I still remember the overwhelming sense of fullness I felt that afternoon as we drove back to the YWAM compound. Later that same afternoon I sat with Antoine and talked about the women. He had been walking with Pastor Ndayizeye for many years, and explained the incredible impact the pastor had had on him and on the entire community.

Another of the projects that Antoine and Moise set up for our team was on the YWAM base. Method and Mary Kamanzi, the founders and directors of the Kigali YWAM base, established a school on the property. In late July of 1994, God called the Kamanzis to move from Uganda to Rwanda. Although they arrived just after the genocide, they told us that the streets were still covered with the evidence of human sin and brutality that motivated the murder of more almost one million innocent men, women, and children. The Kamanzis had been wanting to move back to Rwanda for many years, but the doors remained shut until 1994. They believed that God called them back to be part of the healing of this beautiful nation. To be honest, by the look and feel of Kigali, it seemed that God had called many thousands of people for this same purpose. The Holy Spirit was moving in the city, and we could feel His presence in so many different ways. When the Kamanzis set up the YWAM base, their vision was that the base would become a place of spiritual and emotional healing for the people in the surrounding communities. The elementary school was a key part of this vision.

The aim of the school was to provide a nurturing Christian environment for the many orphans who lived in the local area. The Kamanzi's vision was not to create an orphan school, but a school that mixed the two populations. The Kamanzis saw a great benefit in blending the orphan population with the population of children with parents, and within the first few years of the school's launching, the fruit was unmistakable. They described how strong, healthy families were surrounding the orphaned children with love and care. Many of the families took the more needy children under their own care for different seasons, and they often offered to help the orphanages bear the load of caring for multiple children.

Our service at the school involved setting up an after-school camp. My team of gifted college students broke into four different groups: one group for songs, one group for games, one group for crafts, and one group for an interactive story. The energy in each group was amazing, and as I walked around observing the different teams, it was beautiful to see our team connect with the children in different and dynamic ways. At this camp Sheffield began to exert some leadership in a new and impressive way.

One of the games we played with children involved a series of funny phrases and gestures delivered by one leader. The crowd is required to repeat the funny phrase and imitate the gesture, which becomes a hilarious and wildly silly challenge. I led the first round of the game for a class of about 50 children—the kids love it. We had not seen a response like this in any of our previous camps, and I could tell that Sheffield was particularly energized by the overwhelming response. When I finished the first round, I felt a tug on the tail of my shirt. I looked down and saw Sheffield, his eyes big and bright; he wanted to lead a round of this game. When I introduced him to the students, they cheered encouragement. Sheffield's phrases were clear and his gestures distinct. The students loved him, and they followed with rapt attention. After one round he walked back to stand beside me, his face glowing with joy.

Antoine and Moise introduced us to many more community leaders, and at each project we learned about the different ways that God was moving and rescuing his children in Rwanda. They not only served as our hosts and organizers, but they served beside us, answered our questions, and shared their own stories with us. Because of their incredible generosity of spirit, these two men made special bonds with each of us, including Jack, Naomi, and Sheffield. During our lunch break on our final afternoon, Antoine and Moise told me that they had a surprise for the team. They would meet us in the classroom after our midterm exams, and lead us through one final experience.

This final experience took us to the campus prayer room, which Antoine and Moise had stocked with pillows, blankets, and an assortment of soft, comfortable chairs. They led us in a few worship songs and prayed over our team, thanking God for our friendship, but also praying for the remainder of our travels. After the prayer time, they uncovered buckets of water and told us that they were going to wash our feet. This incredible act of kindness struck me in a special way that night. These two men began washing our feet in the Kigali airport two weeks prior, as they hoisted our bags onto the top of their bus. They washed our feet each day on the base as they helped cook our meals, as they made us coffee, as they set up our schedule, and as they encouraged us with a myriad of kindnesses. This kind of leadership is not common in the world, and we were truly blessed to be served by Antoine and Moise.

Greece:
"Holding the Brick"

In 2015 Greece saw a sudden spike in migrants and asylum seekers as a result of war and deprivation in Syria. The Greek infrastructure was not prepared for the rapid influx and tensions rose across the country from Greek nationals as well as from the struggling migrant communities. During one of the protests, which were breaking out almost daily according to our host Pastor Giotis, a protester hurtled a brick through one of his church's stained-glass windows. Pastor Giotis was in the building at the time of the incident, and he reacted to the destruction in a surprising way. He said, "I went to the sanctuary and picked up the brick. I took it to my office and began to pray. How would God want us to respond to this situation? How would God want us to help and serve those who are most vulnerable?"

Pastor Giotis' concerns were not focused on replacing the expensive damage to his church's historic glass windows. He saw the brick incident as a moment to stop and pray, to reassess priorities, and to follow God into the center of the crisis. "When the brick came through the church window, everything began to change for us," Pastor Giotis explained. He said, "It was not easy to convince our very conservative church body to move into action on behalf of the refugee community, but we have all grown together. I am very proud of the efforts of this very loving community."

One of the church's first major outreach efforts involved taking hundreds of meals into the abandoned airport at Ellinikon, where over forty thousand refugees were living in very desperate conditions. During these visits Pastor Giotis and his team listened to heart-breaking stories of loss and abuse. Many of the refugees had fled from attacking forces in the middle of the night, grabbing only what they could carry. He said, "My eyes were opened at the airport. Refugees are men and women like you and I. I met doctors and lawyers, teachers and social workers; there were so many people who left full, rich lives in order to survive."

These stories motivated Pastor Giotis and his community to purchase several apartment buildings in the Athens area in order to help families start over. These "Homes of Hope" serve families from Syria, Iraq, and Iran. The church also planted several outreach ministries: one multi-cultural church in Exarcheia, an area dominated by one of the largest anarchist communities in Europe, another in Glyfada, and others in the surrounding areas.

After Pastor Giotis' introduction, he invited us to follow him into the fellowship hall. We were met by a wonderful mixture of smells, particularly cardamom, cloves, and saffron. There were about 50 people in the room, and Pastor Giotis encouraged us to spread out among the different tables. He told us that some of the people who attend these weekly dinners are very lonely, still living in wretched conditions without trusted friends to talk with and share life. We could really bless them, Pastor Giotis explained, by listening to their stories and sharing our own.

After Pastor Giotis prayed, he introduced our team, and encouraged his church family to learn about what he called our "wild and crazy world adventure." The energy in the room was full and spirited, with conversations breaking out all around me as different people brought plates of food from the kitchen. Erica and I sat down at a table across from a woman who was surrounded by three little girls. We greeted her and asked about her family. She introduced us to her three daughters, ages 16, 14, and 5. We laughed and told her that our children were the exact same ages. "And your husband, is he here?" I asked. She shook her head and looked down: "He was killed by ISIS forces as we were fleeing Syria." I did not know what to say; this small glimpse into her struggle shocked me into silence. I took a breath, and said, "I am so sorry. I can't imagine." She smiled and said, "Thank you for coming here. This church has been wonderful to us. We were each baptized last week, and we are comforted to know that God is with us, caring for us, and leading us."

She pulled a phone out of her purse and scrolled through some photos. "Here," she said, "these are pictures of our baptism. It was so exciting. We grew up under Islam, and there is no forgiveness in Islam. There is only more work and more struggle. I always felt that there was something more than what I was taught about God. How could a loving God want us to hate one another and to kill one another?" She put her phone back into her purse and put her hand on her little girl's back. She said, "Learning about Jesus Christ changed everything for us. My husband would be so happy. He became a Christian while we were living in Syria, but I was always too afraid to listen." Her 16-year-old daughter, sitting on the other side of the five-year-old, nodded agreement.

Our conversation drifted between the wonderful peace that those in Christ can experience to the love and grace of the church community and even to this woman's experience in the airport refugee camp. She talked about life in Syria before ISIS came to her village. The girls played soccer, went to many school events, and enjoyed afternoon conversations with wonderful neighbors. She said Syrian food was what she most longed for, and that it was impossible to get the same kinds of spices in Athens to replicate the traditional Syrian cuisine. The more we talked, the more I could see myself in her situation. Our families were identical, and the kinds of life activities she described in Syria were the same ones Erica and I and our family enjoyed in America.

At the end of the dinner Pastor Giotis came over and put his hand on my shoulder: "I want you to meet someone." He had a way of always smiling as he spoke. He greeted the lady Erica and I had been speaking with; he knew her name and the names of her three daughters. After saying goodbye to Orhan and her daughters and promising to pray for them, I followed Pastor Giotis across the room.

He led me to a group of men, one of whom was clearly a professional bodybuilder. He put his hand on one of the men and said, "Gentlemen, this is John Norton. He is the leader of the group of college students. I want you to tell him about your ministry. He will have students ready to help in any way." With that, Pastor Giotis stepped back into the crowd. The men smiled at me and introduced themselves: George, Zidane, Amir, Jalm, and the giant Mincha.

George was Pastor Giotis' son, and he led one of the Homes of Hope. Zidane was the leader of the Persian ministry and he also led the weekly Arabic service for the church. Amir, Jalm, and Mincha were Zidane's key leaders in the Persian ministry. Zidane explained that these leaders had only been a part of the church for a few months, but they were strong leaders and wanted to help.

I had dinner with Amir, Jalm, and Mincha a few nights later. We met at the church and walked to a cafe in the Plaka tourist district. As we walked up, I noticed something different about the otherwise gregarious cafe workers, who always put a hand on my shoulder and showed me a menu as I walked by their stores. They turned away as we approached: no smiles, no greeting, no menus. There was one very friendly host, whose cafe I had eaten at a few times, who did not turn away when we approached. I could see concern in his face as he shook my hand, and he seemed reluctant to lead us to a table. I pointed to a table on the patio, and he led us. He gave us some menus and asked about drinks, all the while avoiding eye contact with my companions.

When he walked away, the guys said, "This is one of the problems with life in Greece. We are treated very poorly by most Greeks. Pastor Giotis and the church people are very loving, but out here on the streets it is very dangerous for us each day." They explained the impossibility of finding a job, of finding good places to live, and of building a life in Greece due to the widespread cultural prejudice. Amir said, "I understand that some refugees steal and cause problems, but we are not all the same. We want to live like we did back in Iran, building businesses, making money, and living freely."

Amin went on to describe his life in Iran. He met a Christian through his business, and the truth of the Gospel took hold of his heart. He said, "I knew it was the worst decision I could make for my business and my place in Iranian society. I knew I could be killed for becoming a Christian, but God met me in such a powerful way; I knew His love was real and true, and that I could be forgiven and cared for by Him. I could not deny Him." He shared the Gospel with many people in his family, and they all became Christians too. One of his neighbors was a very militant Muslim, and he told the religious police about Amir. The community around Amir was not radicalized, and although most were Muslims, they did not believe Amir should be killed or imprisoned. A group of his neighbors came to him in the middle of the night, told him about the police, and helped him escape. "One of my friends," Amir said, "drove me several hours to the Turkish border. He could be killed for helping me escape." Jalm nodded and said the same thing happened to him.

Jalm met a group of Christian British students in Iran. When they shared the Gospel with him, he said he felt a weight miraculously lift off his shoulders. "I had been trying to be perfect, as Islam requires, but I could not do it," he explained. "For some reason, I knew that God loved me. Why would He ask me to do something impossible?" When the British students told Jalm that God's law required perfection, like Islam, but that God gave His only Son Jesus Christ as a sacrifice for our sin, he knew it was true. "I had dreams all my life about a man on a cross, but I never knew what these meant. When I shared these dreams with the British students, they got really emotional. They told me this man was Jesus, and that He had been caring for me and loving me all my life." When Jalm told his wife about his conversion, she started to cry. She too had become a Christian, but she was too scared to tell him or anyone else. Jalm and his wife joined an underground church, and after several months of attending, it was raided by the religious police. While these police did not immediately arrest them, Jalm knew they would soon send a van to his home. He would be arrested in the middle of the night, taken away, and killed.

Jalm's wife was not known by the police, so she and their baby daughter were safe from arrest. One of Jalm's friends helped him get to the Turkish border. He would travel to Greece, apply for permanent residence, and send for his wife and daughter. Sadly, at the time of our meeting, this plan had not worked out for Jalm, due to the anti-Iranian sentiments in Greece. "We will need to get out of here if we want to build our lives back," Mincha said.

Mincha toured all around the Middle East and parts of Europe as a professional bodybuilder. He became a Christian after meeting some Christians at a competition in Turkey. The hope of the Gospel slowly worked its way into his heart, and not long after he confessed his faith in Christ, he had been invited to compete in the Iranian national bodybuilding competition. At the national championships he was asked to sign a form declaring that he was a faithful Muslim. "I had signed these forms dozens of times," he said, "but never as a Christian." Mincha wrote "Christian" on the line instead of "Muslim," and at the time no one said anything. A few weeks later, one of his friends in the bodybuilding federation called to warn him that the police were planning to arrest him. Mincha knew his confession was reported to the religious police and that his life was in danger.

He had friends drop him off on the Turkish border, and from there he was transported to a refugee camp in the town called Van. From there Mincha was given special permission to travel to Athens, where he thought he'd have more freedom and opportunities to begin his life again. Mincha waved his hand toward our waiter, who had not returned for 20 minutes to ask about our dinner order. "Here they view me as a threat, as dangerous and suspicious. In Iran I had a beautiful car and a very nice house; I was a celebrity. Now I am nothing." These stories filled me with anger at violent governments, prejudiced people, and the complexity of international immigration worldwide.

We spent the next two hours talking about their lives in Iran and my life in America. As has happened many times in my travels around the world, our conversations made me realize how very similar we are. Their lives growing up in youth sports, school events, and neighborhood activities were all the same as my own. Just as I felt the weight of Orhan's tragic circumstances on my shoulders in the church fellowship hall, I was now feeling the same weight for Amir, Jalm, and Mincha.

As I walked alone back to the Student and Traveler's Inn that night, once again greeted joyfully by all of the cafe merchants, I felt disgusted. My eyes were now open to the fearful prejudice that transformed friendly cafe managers into angry racists. I was more aware than ever of the ways I had been manipulated by an American news media that not only failed to report the most tragic international stories, but twisted world events to fit their own political agendas. I was full of disgust toward my own laziness and at my own overfocus on myself and my own comforts—I was too lazy and self-consumed to listen and to learn about what was going on in some of the most desperate parts of the planet.

Erica and the kids were asleep when I tiptoed into our room. Seeing Erica and each of our kids sleeping peacefully in their beds brought my mind back to Orhan. Because of Pastor Giotis' openness to the voice of God in his life, she and her daughters were sleeping safely in one of the apartments the church had lent them. Because God planted love and compassion in Pastor Giotis's heart,

Orhan and many other families were sleeping in a safe, comfortable place that night. When Pastor Giotis picked the brick up off his sanctuary floor, anger and prejudice could have festered, but God softened his heart, allowing love and compassion to grow.

Germany:
"Church for Sale: $1"

The directions we had followed to the St. Lukas Church (*Lukaskirche*) in Leipzig were about as dizzying as the 19th-century staircases we climbed into the church's bell tower. We rented accommodations at the Hostel Blue Star in Altlindenau, and we traveled by foot, by train, and again by foot to reach the small immigrant-dominant Volkmarsdorf district. Large, dust-brown Cold War-era apartment buildings surround St. Lukas Church and dominate the neighborhood. These ten-story buildings, though imposing in their broad, rectangular strength, seemed to cringe back from the sharp-steepled, bright red-brick church in the center square.

Traveling through a city as a group of 30 has obvious challenges, not to mention the fact that American youth have a way of expanding their presence with personality and enthusiasm. I was never so thankful for our group's size, stamina, and energy as when we reviewed the projects Pastor Hugo Gevers had planned for our team at St. Lukas Church. This massive church was beautiful on the outside, stretching its proud gothic spires into the sky, but on the inside dozens of broken pews were covered in thick dust and various meeting rooms were damp and moldy. There was enough work for 20 teams our size in this church.

As Pastor Hugo led our team through the dusty sanctuary, he pointed at the crumbling walls behind the altar, the rotten wood stacked high in the choir loft, and the cracked flooring all through the massive building. I worried that he had mistaken us for a construction team, and confirmed with my partner Alex Lange about the hours he'd committed our team to work. Alex's eyes were wide; his love for construction had him buzzing with energy and enthusiasm at the opportunities that surrounded us. Alex assured me that the pastor knew we would be working from 1:00-5:00pm each afternoon, but I was still worried about the scope of this project.

Adding to my stress over time was the fact that my colleague and friend Dr. Russell Dawn and his wife Sharon were visiting our team in Germany. Russ had come with a great series of lectures on German history, and I knew he had worked diligently to prepare a compelling curriculum. I wanted to honor Russ' time and expertise, as well as provide the students with adequate time to read, study, and write papers for his classes. I was soon to be assured that Pastor Hugo was not only a thoughtful host, but that he was a loving, fatherly man, determined to care for our team.

We spent our first hour at the St. Lukas Church with Pastor Hugo in a small fellowship room off the transept chapel. The room smelled of fresh-baked cookies, and as Pastor Hugo invited us to sit down, three ladies entered the room with giant trays of sweets. Cookies, sweet cakes, and pie soon covered each of the tables in the room, and as we all gasped at the beautiful sight, Pastor Hugo smiled proudly. He said, "We are very thankful that you are here with us. For many years this church building was owned by the German state. It was originally dedicated in 1893, but since then has faced some very serious opposition. From the Communist Regime to the Nazi Party, not to mention extensive air raids and bombing during World War II, it is a wonder that this incredible building was not destroyed."

Pastor Hugo went on to describe how the church building had fallen into disrepair for many years. When Pastor Hugo and his congregation felt called by God to be a missionary congregation, they began to pray about direction. During this time the German government offered to sell the building to the congregation for one euro, with the understanding that the church would restore the building. The largely German congregation saw this incredible offer as confirmation of their call to be a missionary congregation. They were dedicated to working with the Middle Eastern refugees, largely from Iran and Afghanistan, who lived in the surrounding apartments.

One of the first steps that Pastor Hugo took when the congregation decided to make St. Lukas Church their home was starting an after-school program for the children in the community. He contracted with a company to bring a truckful of tricycles, games, drums, and other big toys to the open area in front of the church each week. Pastor Hugo discovered that many of the children living in the apartments had no safe place to play and no money to purchase these kinds of toys. This weekly play-time event, as well as German language lessons and an after-school tutoring service, were also offered by members of the church. Pastor Hugo described the church transformation with excitement: "These very traditional German Lutherans embraced a massive influx of Persian Muslims, prayed with them, supported them, and encouraged them to join our weekly service. We now have had almost one hundred Persians commit their life to Christ and become Christians." Pastor Hugo smiled and pointed to a 20-something young man in a seat to his right. "This is Daniel, and he is one of my key leaders among the Persian community. He is also my Persian tutor," said Pastor Hugo, and gestured to Daniel to stand and speak to us. Daniel stood and smiled, "Welcome! We are happy to have you here. Maybe we can cook you some nice Persian food while you are here this week." Pastor Hugo put his arm around Daniel's shoulder and nodded, "Oh yes, some of the Persian folks are brilliant cooks. I am sure they would be excited to prepare a meal."

Pastor Hugo eventually divided our team into different groups. Some of us were assigned to tear a thick layer of stucco from the walls around the altar, others to carry thousands of pounds of trash up from a basement, some teammates to clean pews, and others to break down dozens of old, rotten chairs, tables, and bookcases. In the middle of the week, as the dust in the sanctuary was thick enough to slice like strudel, a big box was delivered to the church. Pastor Hugo found me in the fifth-floor spire of the church, close to the bell tower, breaking down one of a dozen old bookshelves. "Dr. Norton, you must come down right away. A big surprise!" he said. By the time I got to the narthex, Pastor Hugo had gathered at least a dozen of my students for the big reveal. He circled the box like it was an undiscovered treasure and said, "Who can guess what this is?" Pastor Hugo looked around at us, but I think we were all a bit stunned. A few of us made guesses along the lines of church sanctuary items, but all were wrong. "Foosball!" he shouted. "Do you know it?" he asked. We all broke down laughing. Pastor Hugo started tearing at the box and said, "The

Persian men love this game, and I want it to be set up right here in the narthex. It will be a huge hit!"

One of the things that made serving with Pastor Hugo truly delightful was his love for people. The notion that this foosball table would bring men from the neighborhood into the church made him nearly dance around us as we finished unpacking the box. He told us about his dream of hosting a foosball tournament and of providing a fun outlet for the hard-working people in his community. He asked me to be in charge of the assembly of the table, and to perhaps give my work in the spire to another student. My son Jack, standing next to me at that moment, was more than happy to be transferred to the demolition crew. A couple of the students stayed with me after hours that day to finish the table, and Pastor Hugo was thrilled. Even as we were putting the final touches on the table, he was walking to the neighboring apartments to announce the completion of the table.

The team of students that I led to Leipzig in the fall of 2017 was a very hard-working team. These young ladies and gentlemen seemed to enjoy it when our hosts told them that there was too much work to complete. These students had a healthy sense of defiance when it came to attacking a job, as they threw themselves into everything. I think their intensity worried Pastor Hugo at times, whose fun-loving, gregarious personality wanted to protect us from over-exertion. He seemed very concerned that we were working too hard. He made rounds, encouraging different groups to take breaks, eat some cake in the fellowship room, and relax for a while.

By the end of our time in Leipzig, we had not only finished all of the projects on Pastor Hugo's list, but he wrote up new plans and added several extra projects. In our final afternoon with Pastor Hugo, he told the team that their hard work had saved the church over $20,000. We all shouted and clapped. It felt so good to be able to join hands in a significant way with this body of international Christians in Leipzig, to be able to sweat and struggle together for a common purpose, and to see the work become a blessing.

On one of our last evenings in Leipzig, the team asked Pastor Hugo if they could have a "movie night" in the fifth-floor spire that we'd cleaned out. He thought it was a great idea. As we climbed the staircase for one of the last times, I remember how dizzying it was to do this for the first time. We had logged dozens of hours in the church, in her spires, and in nearly every corner of the place. We developed a wonderful comfort and a deep sense of connection to the church, which due to Pastor Hugo's welcoming spirit, had become for us a true home of worship.

PART 6

ATW 2019

Although in 2016 we planned to run the ATW program every year, without Adam Lee on the team, this plan did not work out logistically. Our 2017 team returned to campus with a lot of energy for ministry and campus outreach. It is always a delight to watch the ATW students hit campus with a heightened desire to serve and to learn.

As my key partner on the ATW 2017 semester, Alex not only earned my respect as a skilled leader, he also caught the attention of the university. A few months after we returned to campus, he was hired to assist Faith McKinney as a full-time staff member in the Global Programs Office.

Preparations for the sixth ATW Semester began in January of 2018. We employed a new structure for the 2019 trip. Erica and I would serve as the primary leaders, and we would have four visiting professors. Throughout the semester Alex Lange provided budget management and logistical support from home, but he and Anne also visited us and provided extra assistance while we traveled through Greece and Israel.

Leadership Team:
John and Erica Norton*
Dr. Bryan Santin, visiting professor in China
Dr. Jack Schultz, visiting professor in Mongolia
Dr. Mike Middendorf, visiting professor in Greece and Israel
Dr. Caleb Karges, visiting professor in Hungary and Austria
Alex and Anne Lange, logistical support in Greece and Israel

Josh Foss (GA)   Nyssa McCarthy (GA)
Laura Mietzner (GA)   Christian Woodfin (GA)
*The Norton children: Jack (17), Naomi (15), Sheffield (6)

Student Team:

Carter Annema	Sam Beeson
Natalie Bergler	Kaylin Brand
Jonah Clausen	Kathryn Clausen
Kaylee De La Motte	Jarrett Donham
Grace Grant	Effie Hill
Ryan Jones	Alec Leissring
Hannah Loesch	Jonathan Luna
Nathan MacGregor	Jacob Manning
Lillian Niccum	Kessler O'Brien
Chloe Read	Hannah Rost
Reese Rountree	Hannah Scheyder
Kirstie Schierkolk	Ava Schweninger
Lucas Senkbeil	Seth Skogerboe
Nathan Smith	Savannah Stame
Khoi Vu	Payton Walter

Itinerary:

China—Mongolia—Vietnam—Nepal—India—Malta—Greece—Israel—
Uganda—Hungary—Austria—Spain—Costa Rica

China:
"Roads in Deserts, Streams in Thirsty Lands"

We stepped out of the dry, air-conditioned bus into a wall of thick, wet air. The humidity soaked my t-shirt in those first few minutes outside the bus, but I loved it. Heat and humidity make for great discomfort, but in the courtyard of the Mariner's Harbor Children's Village in Tianjin, they helped to serve up a sweet sense of nostalgia. While my students collected their backpacks, I took a moment to face the compound and take it all in. Two weeks and two years earlier, I stood in this courtyard with tears running down my face. We fell in love with this incredible ministry that offered sweet, loving care and world-class medical services to children with special needs.

This sweet moment of nostalgia brought all those emotions back, but I knew there was a tragic difference. During our two-year absence from the Mariner's Harbor Home, a devastating new Chinese law resulted in the emptying of the homes and required all of the children to be sent away. Sweeping new reforms forced all of the children at Mariner's Harbor to be relocated to orphanages in the towns where they were born.

One of the reasons founder, Tim Butler, established Mariner's Harbor was to provide special care for special children, care these kids were not getting anywhere else. One of the amazing things I first heard about Tim was that he was like a Major League scout. He sought out children with special needs from all over China. He put together a world-class team and built an incredible facility for his awesome "recruits." Many of the children that Mariner's Harbor targeted had severe disabilities, some requiring simple surgeries and others more complex operations. In more simple orphan homes, many of these children did not receive the care they needed. Some children were resigned to extreme dis-comfort, while others endured torturous and life-threatening situations. Instead of being relegated to back rooms or left untreated in lonely orphanage beds, Butler's recruits were given high-quality care. From surgeries, therapy, specially designed education, and loving attention, Tim and his Mariner's Harbor team created a place where these children could thrive.

Since my previous visit in 2017 all of the children were gone and the four large family homes were empty. The bustling energy in each home, the funny and affectionate house mothers, the sweet little faces—all gone. When our hosts John and Heidi gave our 2019 team a tour of the facility, I felt like I was walking through a war zone. Empty beds and broken toilets, flooring ripped up and walls broken down, a renovation project was well under way, but all I could see was a sad emptiness.

I took some time one afternoon to sit on the floor of the empty house where I first met a boy named Zander. Befriending this young man and work-ing with him in 2017 impacted my heart in a significant way. I reflected that afternoon about the tremendous damage caused by short-sighted government policies, and a government that moved quickly without the proper checks and balances of a voting public. One of the staff members who helped organize our stay in 2017, and who was once again hosting us and caring for us, was an American woman named Naomi. She shared about how painful it was to see the children taken away. She said, "We cried every day as we watched our children get lifted into government buses or vans. It was a much different thing to see a little boy or girl get adopted. We missed them, but we knew they were entering a loving home where they would be covered in affection by their adoptive par-ents. This was different." The Mariner's Harbor staff knew that some of their precious children would be relocated in rundown facilities where they would be neglected. Very few of the simpler government homes were set up to help the children grow and develop. In the midst of this tremendous tragedy, Tom Butler got a new vision for Mariner's Harbor.

Butler's new vision provided a solution for one of China's shortsighted, inhumane policies pertaining to orphaned children, the "age-out" law. All orphaned children are cared for and supported by the Chinese government until they turn 14, after which they are expected to care for themselves. While some of the orphaned children prove ready and able to support themselves when they turn 14, many of the kids with more significant needs are not. The age-out law does not take into consideration the fate of these special children. Tragically, these kids are either pushed out into apartments alone or they are committed to homes for the elderly. Neither of these options is suitable, and according to Naomi many end up in very unhealthy situations.

Tim Butler's new vision for his empty facility involved caring for and providing occupational therapy for a growing population of aged-out kids with more severe needs. Butler explained, "Tragically, the Chinese government doesn't care what happens to these kids, but we do." Tim and his team were enthusiastic about welcoming more than 25 new residents into the Mariner's Harbor community. "We will provide necessary surgeries and ongoing therapy for these older kids, too. That part of our original vision will not change," Butler explained. Because the new residents are adults, the Mariner's Harbor homes required significant renovation. Once outfitted with tiny toilets, sinks, cribs, and beds for babies and small children, Mariner's Harbor would now require everything adult-sized.

While it was sad to see the empty beds and quiet rooms, our 2019 team of university students loved supporting the new vision. Our team was one of the first groups that would prepare the facility for this major transition. The work involved retrofitting each of the homes into a place where teens and young adults could live. Cribs and diaper stations were replaced by bunk beds, desks, and adult-sized sinks and toilets. The floors and open spaces were reshaped to accommodate larger residents, which involved taking down walls and replacing flooring. Our team engaged in almost all of these new projects, as well as many landscaping projects. By 5:00pm each day we were all dripping in sweat. We worked with vision and excitement, knowing our labor was helping to create a newly renovated space for some really special young adults.

During our two weeks at Mariner's Harbor in 2019 we built a friendship with our hosts Naomi, John, and Heidi. We ate meals with them and enjoyed their company immensely. As our time was coming to a close, I asked Naomi and John and Heidi to share their stories with us. How did they end up at

Mariner's Harbor? How had God convinced them to move to Tianjin and to join this incredible ministry? They each shared very powerful stories of God's faithfulness. When Heidi finished sharing, she looked around the room at all of us. She thanked us for our work and for really giving ourselves to some tough projects. Her husband John jumped in and thanked the landscape team for hauling dirt and bricks and so much more. Heidi said, "You guys worked really hard, but your biggest gift to us was your friendship and kindness. You expressed genuine enthusiasm for our new vision, and your daily partnership blessed us." With this she started to break down, and we all started crying with her. She continued, "I mean, who cares about the friggin' dirt?! You blessed us each day with your kind faces and with your willingness to engage in friendly conversations." Heidi's statement impacted our team, and her words were repeated and re-pondered throughout that semester of travel. I can't even count how many times God used that phrase to help correct our course, our focus, and our attitudes. "Who cares about the friggin' dirt" became a mantra for us, reminding us that people must always be valued and cared for above projects.

On our final day in Tianjin, I loaded my backpack onto our bus and turned to face the Mariner's Harbor compound. I noticed that several of my students struck the same posture. Leaving this place was never going to be easy. I looked back at the four homes and imagined all the bunk beds, the living rooms, and the kitchens full of life and energy. I imagined the playground and the weight room, the computer lab and the classrooms noisy with learning and growth. This vision brought to my mind Isaiah 43:19, "I am creating something new. There it is! Do you see it? I have put roads in deserts, streams in thirsty lands." God was doing something new and exciting at Mariner's Harbor, and we all felt blessed to be one small part of His vision for this wonderful place.

Mongolia: "We Saved the Eyeball for You, Professor"

"We saved the eyeball for you, professor!"

I forced a smile and looked at Dr. Schultz, my professor colleague. He cracked a sly smile and raised his eyebrows. My stomach tightened at the thought of swallowing the rubbery ball of white flesh that hung from our host's fork.

Rewind two weeks.

My wife Erica and I dreamed of riding horses across the Mongolian plains for many years. As often happens with dreams, this exotic equestrian experience would require much more of us than we expected. Our dream was realized when we landed in Mongolia in the fall of 2019. We rented a pack of 40 horses and rode as a team for five hours through Terelj National Park. Green rolling hills, sharp rocky outcroppings, and vast sweeping plains—at times it was difficult to concentrate on controlling my bouncy, curious horse in this breathtaking landscape.

The extreme beauty of Mongolia is matched by the extreme rigor required of those who call it home. Boasting one of the coldest average temperatures in the world, Mongolia is no horse trot. Mongolians must seriously plan for the winter months, which are violent, harsh, and unfruitful. The extreme weather even required early Mongolian peoples to design a diet that prepared them for the intense winter cold and frozen months of scarce resources. For instance, in summer the early Mongolian people groups loaded up on dairy products, and in winter they ate more meat and animal fat. This extra fat served to keep them warmer as wild winds slipped under the bright orange doors of their gers—circular tents similar to Russian yurts. While traces of this traditional diet can be found in the habits of twenty-first century Mongolians, modern technology allows them more dietary freedoms.

David and Rachel Jones were our missionary hosts in Mongolia. They invited our team to serve in their Mongolian ministry, but we soon discovered that there was nothing Mongolian about the Jones family. Originally from the American Midwest, the Jones were first called to serve in Kazakhstan, where they preached and established churches for eight years. It was for the Kazakh people that the Jones felt a deep connection and affection, but with growing tensions toward Christian outreach in Kazakhstan, the Jones were forced to leave.

Although heartbroken to leave a land they had grown to love, the Jones did not give up. They discovered that many Kazakh Christians were relocating to Mongolia. In fact, the largest population of Kazakhs outside of Kazakhstan is in Mongolia. Determined to follow the call of God in their lives, the Jones followed the Kazakh trail to Ulaanbaatar where David, an ordained teacher and pastor in the Lutheran church, began training Kazakh Christians in Mongolia for pastoral ministry.

Pastor Jones and Rachel introduced our team to a few of the wonderful Kazakh pastors they had helped train for ordination. These courageous men and their families journeyed into Christian ministry through what seemed impossible cultural obstacles. Many had been rejected by their families and friends for turning against Islam, yet these Kazakh Christians were convinced of the gospel truth.

One of the Kazakh pastors who served with the Jones family was a long-time farmer. This was a man who David believed would serve as a wonderful instructor for our team of students. "Pastor James can teach your team about the way Kazak Mongolians live today," David explained, and so we made a plan to have James come to our ger camp.

Pastor James arrived with two white sheep in the back of his Toyota pickup truck. We were staying at a ger camp about two hours outside of Ulaanbaatar in the Terelj National Park. Before James' arrival, David told my six-year-old son Sheffield that Pastor James would be showing us how Kazakhs prepare a sheep for dinner. Sheffield was thrilled at the idea, and when the truck arrived, he sprinted after it. It was Sheffield's seventh birthday that day, and he was delighted to use his birthday privilege to stand in the front row for the slaughter.

When Pastor James slit the first sheep's throat, Sheffield leaned over to see the blood collect in a silver tin. When James pulled the guts from inside the sheep, Sheffield knelt in the grass beside him to get a closer look at the intestines and organs. When one of James' helpers held up the sheep's lungs by the trachea, blew into the trachea, and filled the lungs like bloody balloons, Sheffield stepped up and said, "Can I try that?" Without hesitation the farmer handed Sheffield the trachea. I lifted my hand and stepped toward Sheffield, but in one fluid motion he grabbed the fleshy rope and pressed his lips to the open pipe. I froze. Erica held a hand to her open mouth to muffle a scream. Sheffield blew the lungs full, and the lifeless bags took full shape beneath his command. Our team of college students erupted with applause and cheers. Sheffield smiled with bloody lips and passed the trachea to his big brother Jack.

I stood beside David for most of this preparation, and he and James related some very interesting details about Kazakh sheep slaughtering. David explained how each organ, each piece of the intestine, and even all of the sheep's bones would be put to use by a typical Kazakh family. Not only were special dishes created to feature different parts of the sheep, but Kazak families also tanned the hides for clothing and furniture, sharpened bones for tools, and even collected the sheep knuckles to play a popular children's game. There was a deep respect for animals in both Kazakh and Mongolian cultures, and each creature was cherished for the way it helped sustain a family.

The eyeball that my host extended to me exemplified the Kazakh and Mongolian faithful care of the land. From farming to husbandry, these people understand scarcity and operate with a purpose to use every piece of land and every part of an animal. Thoughts of honor, hospitality, and gratitude swept over my mind as I stared at the skewered eyeball. These Mongolian and Kazakh hosts cared for us, instructed us, and invited us to participate in some very important traditions. They opened their lives and their land to us, and eating the eyeball was one small way to express my gratitude for their kindnesses.

I took the fork, tried to bite off a small piece of the eyeball, and realized it was very tough and very rubbery. Instead of making a scene, I slurped it up, took one hard bite, and swallowed it whole. As the ball of rubbery flesh made its slow journey down my esophagus, four or five different hands clapped my back. I turned to see Pastor James, David, and several of our hosts smiling with pride.

Vietnam: "Fighting for Friendship"

As the son of a Vietnam War veteran, I imagined that I would encounter many things in Vietnam that would disturb me. In Ho Chi Minh City I was told that our team must visit a famous museum called the War Remnants Museum. Some quick research about the museum convinced me that the facility was an example of government deception and social manipulation. The original name for this facility was The Museum of Chinese and American War Crimes. Although the title on the structure was changed in recent years, my research informed me that the content and the story told by the museum had not changed.

I entered the museum with my family and a few students. The main court-yard of the museum was like a cemetery of confiscated United States military equipment. Army helicopters and tanks, Air Force planes and fighters, and dozens of surface-to-air missile launchers decorate the main courtyard of the museum. I felt like I was walking on enemy ground as we toured the grounds, examining what seemed to me like stolen American machinery.

We worked our way into the first floor of the museum, where anti-American propaganda covered every wall. The museum tells a dramatic, one-sided story of American aggression in Vietnam. No mention of a Vietnamese Civil War, nor of North Vietnamese aggression, is mentioned in the museum. Like many of the Vietnamese citizens who visit the museum, an ignorant observer would leave the museum imagining that the United States attacked Vietnam to simply pillage the country of her resources. The museum artifacts, pictures, and posters communicated that it was a greedy American empire that started the Vietnam War. The message promoted by the museum was loud and clear: it was the heroics of Ho Chi Minh that repelled the American aggressor, ultimately leading Vietnam to peace, unity, and prosperity.

My son Jack and I walked together up to the second floor of the museum, both of us full of frustration at the intense propaganda that unfairly incriminated the United States and failed to honor the real history. On the second floor everything changed. The frustration I felt from reading the propaganda on the first floor dissipated as I examined the museum's second-floor displays. The artifacts here told a story about the devastation caused by a US military program called Operation Ranch Hand. While the museum reported incorrectly about why the US used Agent Orange, the tragedy of this chemical's use is far greater than the propaganda surrounding it.

The sad story behind the use of Agent Orange began with the need for the US military to stop the invading North Vietnamese forces. With the benefit of thick rainforests and challenging jungle terrain, the attacking North Vietnamese troops had a significant advantage over the US ground troops. Agent Orange was apparently only intended to defoliate the jungle, but a chemical called dioxin was created during production. Only after spraying more than 11 million gallons of dioxin-laced Agent Orange did the US government admit that it had been poisoning its own troops as well as millions of Vietnamese people.

Short term exposure to this horrifying chemical can cause liver problems, nerve disorders, muscular dysfunction, hormone disruption, and heart disease. It has also come to light that the kind of Agent Orange the US government sprayed all over Vietnam will survive in the soil for decades. Women who come into contact with the contaminated soil pass the toxins along to children in the womb, causing miscarriages, spina bifida, and other problems with fetal brain and nervous system development.

As I walked around the second floor of the War Remnants Museum, I was struck by a heart-breaking truth. While the Vietnamese government was guilty of pumping truck loads of mind-bending propaganda into their citizenry, the US government was guilty of using an untested and highly dangerous chemical to fight the North Vietnamese. The repercussions of this decision continue to bear a tragic harvest in Vietnam today, more that 50 years after Agent Orange was deployed.

Shortly after our troubling visit to the War Remnants Museum, we were invited to serve with an organization that was established by veterans from the Vietnam War called Friendship Village. This organization was supported by veterans from American, South Vietnamese, and North Vietnamese regiments. The Friendship Village compound was located about an hour by bus from central Hanoi in a rural community surrounded by a thick jungle. The front gates were tall and freshly painted, and the campus was well-manicured, giving every sign of regular care and thoughtful maintenance.

We met our host, Mrs. Nguyen, in a giant board room, and it was here that we were given an introduction and some of the background information of this organization. Establishment of the Friendship Village was initiated by a group of American GIs who hoped to provide assistance for Vietnamese citizens who had been affected by Agent Orange.

"American GIs established this organization to provide medical care and therapy, not only for their military rivals, but for their children," Mrs. Nguyen explained. "For many years now, groups of American and Vietnamese veterans visit this facility annually for reunions. They work together to keep this place running," she said. These stories had a deep impact on our team, as we had been reading about the Vietnam War and discussing the tragedies of large-scale international conflicts. Additionally, many of us had been deeply troubled by what we witnessed in the War Remnants Museum regarding the US government's use of Agent Orange.

After our introduction, Mrs. Nguyen led us to the Friendship Village school. The school was created to provide vocational training and other special education for children with disabilities caused by Agent Orange. We walked through several of the school's classrooms, witnessing first hand the devastation of chemical warfare, yet enjoying some wonderful interactions with the students. Some of the very young kids were learning to read and write, while some of the older ones were learning to sew, learning woodworking, and learning to create sellable handicrafts.

The kindness and joy of these children had a really powerful impact on me and on many of my students. In spite of some very severe disabilities, the young people at Friendship Village were learning and growing, putting great efforts into developing new skills and trades that would help them move toward greater independence and freedom. It was really powerful to witness.

After our inspiring interactions in the school, we walked to a large meeting room to hear from a group of 20 veterans. These were men who had fought on behalf of the North Vietnamese army. I had mixed emotions as I followed Mrs. Nguyen to the meeting room. My own grandfather and father, as well as my pastor had all fought in the Vietnam War. They told me some pretty gruesome stories about the horrors of this war, and I was about to sit with the enemy. My feelings of patriotic allegiance were mixed with an unsettling sense of guilt caused by seeing the generational effects of my country's use of Agent Orange on these men and on their families.

After we had taken our seats, forming a large circle, the Vietnam veterans entered the room. They were old men, some limping slowly, others walking with deliberate grace and strength. They took seats in such a way as to honor a few leaders above the rest. There was still a strong measure of respect among these men, and they deferred to those who had held a higher rank in the military. When Mrs. Nguyen asked them to share a bit about themselves, the group looked at one man in particular to start the introductions. This gentleman explained that they were all veterans of a very sad war. He told us that although America was once their chief enemy, they now considered America a friend. He was honored to call many American GIs his personal friends and his partners in a great cause that they were celebrating right here at the Friendship Village.

It was moving to hear stories of forgiveness and of new life. Many of these men still suffered from wounds incurred in battle, yet they each had a new vision for life. Some described how they were once required to kill and take life, but after the war they felt a compelling responsibility to give life and help others walk into a brighter future. They were all very happy to be able to call America a friend, and one they were happy to now join hands with for healing purposes.

Although we would have stayed with the men longer, they had to leave us in order to prepare for their annual reunion with a group of American GIs who were arriving for lunch. I would have loved to see that reunion and to hear some of those conversations too. As we walked back to our bus something came together in my mind. While the Vietnam War was terrible on so many different levels, it was in the past. That conflict is part of our painful history, but the fighting is over. The work we are called to now is one that involves reconciliation and reconstruction. Stewing in anger and mistrust only slows our progress toward a better future. The North Vietnamese veterans and their partnership with the American GIs show us that we can do great things when we move forward with humility, forgiveness, and friendship.

Israel:
"Still a Holy Land"

The Wailing Wall, Hezekiah's Tunnel, the Temple Mount, the Mount of Olives, and many more popular sites were on our itinerary through Israel, yet there was one moment at one shoreline that surpassed them all. This event, which happened neither in Jerusalem nor in the shadow of any great monument, stands as a beautiful testimony of God's enduring love and care for his children.

We started our adventure in Caesarea, a coastal city north of Tel Aviv. Many consider the impressive harbor in Caesarea, designed and built by Herod the Great, one of the greatest works of architectural genius in the Ancient Near East. This ancient city was the home of Philip the Evangelist, written about in Acts 8 and 21. The apostle Peter traveled to Caesarea to minister to a Roman centurion named Cornelius, in Acts 10, and the apostle Paul spent time here too as a prisoner.

My friend and colleague Dr. Middendorf, a Bible scholar and archeologist, led us through Israel and Palestine. Dr. Middendorf explained that some people call a visit to the Holy Land "the fifth gospel." He explained, "Journeying through these places will allow you to read the scriptures with new eyes, gaining new clarity about the settings, and gifting you with new mental color and detail."

Our time in Israel involved visiting Nazareth, where we toured a reconstruction of a first-century town called "Nazareth Village." This tour gave us some wonderful images of first-century life, complete with a biblical meal including fresh fire-baked flatbread, lentil soup, za'atar dip (ground hyssop, sesame seeds, and olive oil), hummus dip, labneh dip (a soft cheese made from strained yogurt), olives, salad, and apple slices with date spread.

After Nazareth we climbed Mount Tabor to visit the site where Jesus was transfigured in the miraculous presence of Moses and Elijah. This hike up Tabor was supposed to be a light hike, but it turned out to be very difficult and very steep. We were motivated to make it happen, and when we finally reached the summit we visited the church and spent some time praying and worshiping as a team. Our journey down the mountain was dark and treacherous, but by God's grace we slipped and tripped to our bus without injury. I can still hear Dr. Middendorf citing his tour book in a sarcastic tone: "The hike up Mt. Tabor is just light work!"

Bethsaida, where Jesus called the first disciples, Capernaum, where Jesus preached in the synagogue, and the Mount of Beatitudes all proved to be wonderful places to visit, read scripture, and pray. We traveled south to explore Qumran, where the Dead Sea Scrolls were discovered. We ascended Masada to see the ruins of Herod's incredible palace and to hear the tragic story of the mass suicide that took place there at the end of the first Jewish-Roman War of 74 AD. We floated on the Dead Sea and eventually ascended to Jerusalem, where we visited many incredible sites: David's palace, Hezekiah's Tunnel, the Pool of Siloam, the Wailing Wall, the Church of the Holy Sepulcher, and the Garden of Gethsemane. We toured Jerusalem, visiting the famous Garden Tomb and walking the Via Dolorosa.

On Sunday morning we traveled from Jerusalem to Bethlehem. We worshiped at the Christmas Lutheran Church and met with Pastor Mitri Raheb, who hosted us for a wonderful lunch at the church. Pastor Raheb gave our team a lecture on the Palestinian-Israeli conflict. He told many heart-breaking stories about the ways the Israeli government daily threatens the well-being of innocent Palestinian citizens, and how living inside of a walled city has become more and more like a prison for him, for his family, and for their church congregation. We prayed for Pastor Raheb, and it was faith-building to see his great hope and far-reaching vision for the Palestinian people.

Our time in Israel transformed my personal study of the Bible. When I read the Scriptures now, Old and New Testaments, I picture the topography and sense the distances and elevations. Dr. Middendorf's teachings helped erect ancient homes and temples in my mind. His teaching and storytelling made real cities and towns out of the protected ruins of each historical location. At each site he read from the Scriptures, making direct connections between the text and the site. We walked where Jesus walked, and we traveled where the heroes of our faith traveled.

More than any of these sites, one event during our time in Israel put a new accent and vivid new detail on my belief in God's goodness and mercy. One of my students, Effie Hill, asked if she could be baptized in the Sea of Galilee. She made this request of me six weeks before our arrival in Israel, and I consented without thinking about it. When we arrived in Israel I mentioned it to Dr. Middendorf. He put his hand on my shoulder and nodded slowly. "Oh, that would be something very special. That would be wonderful," he said, looking straight into my face. "We could do that at the Ein Gev kibbutz," he said, and I could tell that he was beginning to plan the details in his mind.

When we arrived at the kibbutz our hosts gave us a brief introduction and showed us each to our different accommodations. The boys stayed in a dormitory, the girls in a bunk house, and the Middendorfs, Erica, Sheffield, and I in an apartment that once served as the changing rooms for the kibbutz theater. Our rooms were funky, but they were clean and the beds were comfortable. The best part about our apartment was that it was located right next to the Sea of Galilee. On our first morning at the kibbutz, I rose early and went for a swim in the sea. The water was perfect, mid-seventies and calm. I swam for a few hundred yards parallel to the shore, aware from my Bible reading that storms can kick up on the Sea of Galilee at a moment's notice. When I came out of the water, Dr. Middendorf walked up with a towel under his arm. "Boker tov!" he shouted, a "good morning" greeting in Hebrew. He pointed to the beach and said, "What do you think about this spot here for Effie's baptism?" There was plenty of room for the team to gather on the edge of the water, and this area would allow us to stand waste deep in the water without walking too far from the shore. "I love it," I said, "I think this will be really special." It wasn't until I was standing beside Effie and Dr. Middendorf three days later, that I knew how special this baptism would truly be.

As the three of us stood waist deep in the Sea of Galilee, facing our team, Dr. Middendorf described baptism as a gift from God, not simply a ritual or symbol, but a powerful means of grace by which God grants faith and the forgiveness of sins. He asked Effie if she believed that Jesus is Lord, that he died on the cross to pay the penalty for her sins, and that God raised him from the dead. With tears in her eyes, Effie said, "Yes, I believe." With that Dr. Middendorf asked if she wanted to be baptized. Again, she said yes, and he said, "Effie Hill, I baptize you in the name of the Father, and of the Son, and of the Holy Spirit," and we lowered her back into the water and then up onto her feet. Even now as I write this I feel a tightening in my chest. My eyes were full of tears that day when we lifted Effie up out of the water, and still today the memory is precious to me. I saw faith in Effie's eyes when she hugged me, and I knew that faith was the greatest gift of God to any man or woman.

"For God so loved the world," that at the perfect time in history, he sent his only Son, Jesus Christ, to be born into the world. Jesus would be born of a woman in the Roman-occupied land of Israel in the first century. He would walk along the shores of Galilee, and he would even walk on top of the water in which we baptized Effie. Jesus would draw fish out of this sea and eat it with his friends on this shore. He would create parables and other teachings about our Heavenly Father that related directly with these mountains and hills, the land and the water that surrounded this place. And then he would travel for days and days, finally ascending to the city of Jerusalem, where he knew he would be crushed by the sins of the whole world. These sins would slash and cut him; they would pierce his flesh, and they would pin him to a cross where he would gasp for air until his life was no more. His body would be laid in a tomb, and although guarded by soldiers, in three days the tomb would be opened and he would rise, alive and restored. Effie's baptism, framed by an ancient backdrop of historical, incarnational love, was a powerful reminder that our Heavenly Father is still raising the dead and restoring the lives of his children, through Jesus Christ our Lord.

Uganda: "Plowing into Discomfort"

Godfrey is built like an NFL running back. His shoulders, thick and muscular, could bust through most any defensive line. Born in Uganda and employed by the Youth with a Mission team in Jinja, his brawn is being employed for the protection of children and others who cannot protect themselves. One group of children that is particularly dear to Godfrey resides at the Home of Hope, a home for children with special needs.

The drive from the YWAM base to the Home of Hope took us through the rural outskirts of Jinja. Although the roads to the home were more fit for horses, goats, and small motorcycles, Godfrey's skilled driving allowed us to move safely around many obstacles. Giant ruts cut into the road by violent rainstorms made sections of the road nearly impassable. Godfrey drove in a zig-zag pattern, back and forth, across the narrow country roads, sometimes nearly stopping to keep the van from bottoming out.

Godfrey is not a talkative person, but in between bumps he said, "We are going to a very special place. The woman who started the home is very strong. We will have her tell you her life story." I nodded and said, "Hearing stories about God's grace is always really wonderful." Godfrey shook his head and smiled, "I don't think you've ever heard anything like Edith's story." With that, he pointed to the right side of the road, indicating that we had arrived.

Tall iron gates locked together with a thick chain stood between us and a four-acre compound. Through the bars I saw three children swinging on a playground, four others sat and waved at our van from an open porch. Godfrey told us to wait in the van while he unbolted the gate and swung it into the playground.

A woman in a pressed business suit met us on the porch of a small, white home. She shook our hands as we filed into the main hallway. Clean wooden floors, brightly painted walls, and the broad smile of a little boy in a wheelchair greeted us as we waited for Edith's instructions. The little boy rolled up beside me and took my hand. He said his name was Tom, and that he was ten years old. I smiled and told him I was John, and that I was 48 years old. This information made him giggle. "That's pretty old," he said. I reached for his armpit, but he was too quick and rolled toward the front door. As Edith passed him, she caressed his head and told us to "watch out for Tom." He smiled back at us and headed out to the playground.

Edith stood in the middle of our group and welcomed us again. After asking for our names and where each of us was from, she told us that God had helped her set up the Home of Hope in the face of some serious opposition. She had a son named Derrick in 2000, and within days of his birth he began to have severe medical problems. He was diagnosed with malaria in his first week of life, and perhaps due to the challenges placed on his immune system, he contracted meningitis. Edith explained, "Derrick started getting convulsions on and off, and he developed a breathing problem. We stayed in the hospital with him for two months, because he needed to be on oxygen." Edith described the physical challenges Derrick faced as a result of the brain damage he incurred from meningitis. These physical challenges, though severe, were nothing compared to the social challenges that Edith soon faced on account of his disabilities. As Edith hunted for hospitals and schools that offered resources for Derrick, she felt pushback from many in her community who believed he was bewitched. Many claimed Edith was cursed for giving birth to a child with disabilities. These harmful stigmas did not stop her.

In 2004, Edith's prayers for support were answered when a non-profit organization focusing on children with disabilities started up in her town. Through this organization, Spring of Hope, Edith not only received help for Derrick, but she was able to meet many other struggling families. The Spring of Hope leadership recognized Edith's great love for children, and they asked her to join their team. Edith explains some of the heart-breaking things she discovered while working with Spring of Hope on her website. She writes,

> They wanted me to work in the community visiting parents who had children with disabilities, encouraging them and teaching them how to do exercises with their children. I took the offer! When I started working in the community I found that many children with disabilities were abandoned and left in the villages with "old grannies." When a child has a visible physical disability, some parents don't want to be seen with such children in public. Because of these powerful stigmas, some parents are pressured to give the children to the "old grannies" in the village to take care of them. As a result of overburdening the older women, the kids do not receive good care. The children in this situation develop terrible bed sores and they are very malnourished. Other parents lock their children inside their houses, where many die of hunger. It was really hard for me to work with the grandmothers, because they had so many kids to care for. These older women had a massive workload, and they could not do much to help the children develop and grow.

It was at this time, while working for Spring of Hope and discovering the incredible need for more resources, that Edith began to feel God's call on her life. He called her to care for more children. She denied the call at first, unable to imagine having the energy to extend herself beyond caring for Derrick. Edith was on her way to work one morning when she was hit by a car. Edith suffered a spinal cord fracture and a pelvic fracture, and the doctors told her that she would never walk again.

Edith described to us how she pleaded with God, promising to open a home for the children if he allowed her to walk. She smiled, pointed to her healthy legs, and said, "He heard my prayer." With the help of some wonderful friends from New Zealand, Edith received funding not only for her hospital care but also for the Home of Hope. She opened the home in 2007 with Derrick and five other children. As we stood in the main hall of the Home of Hope, Edith and her team were offering care to 60 children, all of whom were at one time abandoned or severely neglected.

In addition to providing a home, schooling, and therapeutic care for children, Edith and her team do community education work. They teach parents that the popular stigmas are false, and they help parents see how every child is a gift from God. Her team provides coaching on the best practices of caring for children with disabilities, with the goal of reducing the numbers of abandoned children.

While Edith was speaking, Godfrey was standing behind her smiling and nodding. As she finished speaking, he wiped some tears from his eyes and put his hand on her shoulder. He said to our group, "This is a brave woman. She has changed this entire village, and many people in the city have been influenced by her love." Edith smiled and told us that one of her biggest challenges is staffing. She needs more hands to hug and hold the children, and so this was our job that afternoon. For the next two hours my team spread out across the facility and hugged babies, some not more than four months old. Some of my team members played games with the older kids, which led to some funny conversations and much laughter. I sat in a room full of infants, some wiggling on blankets, some rolling or crawling, and others learning to stand. A few of these children had very slight disabilities, others had major challenges.

At the end of our time at the home I found Godfrey sitting on the porch with a little boy. He was playing a funny hand-slap game, and making the little boy burst with laughter. When I sat down next to him, he introduced me to Moses. Moses was four years old, and he had tight, white braces on his legs. Godfrey explained that Moses had required several surgeries on his legs and that he was finally learning to walk as a four-year-old. Moses demonstrated his ability to grab the porch railing and to stand up. He took three proud steps before falling into my chest. His broad grin made me realize that he'd fallen strategically, trying to tackle me. I poked his ribs, and he laughed and curled up tightly. When I pulled him in for a hug, Godfrey reached over and rubbed Moses' back. "This guy is talented," Godfrey said, "He's gonna be a great teacher someday, I think." A beautiful vision seemed to pass across Godfrey's face. Perhaps he could see an opening in the defensive line and was preparing to provide some lead blocking for young Moses.

Hungary:
"Dancing with Bence"

We met Bence on our first full day in Győr. He bounced to a beat inside his own head, and he seemed interested to connect with others and to share the music of his giant personality. Because of his generous spirit, Bence got behind the programs our team offered to the students at the Peterfy Sandor Evangelical School (PSE). Bence not only encouraged fellow students and friends to join our classes, but he served our team with translation, cultural advice, and most importantly kind friendship as we explored Győr. This beautiful city, located halfway between Budapest and Vienna, was the wealthiest city we visited on our 14-country, around-the-world adventure. As I shook Bence's hand, I wondered what our team could offer a wealthy, educated community like this one. Bence's family, like many of the families in his community, did not seem to have any apparent needs. As Christmas cheer began to spread out over Győr, a new clarity about people began to form in my heart.

Our host in Győr was a former student of mine at Concordia. Sarah was an English major during my first few years of teaching at Concordia; she was a strong young scholar, energetic and mission minded. In 2004, when I announced to her class that I would be forming a small weekly prayer group, Sarah was the first to join. It was clear back then that Sarah was serious about her faith in Christ and that she wanted to share the Gospel with others. I was not surprised when, after graduation, Sarah became a missionary teacher at a Christian school in Győr.

Almost two decades later, it was a great delight to meet up with Sarah, her husband Tamas, and their children in Győr. We were thrilled to be able to serve with Sarah and her team at the Christian school that hired her after college. We arrived in Győr by bus from Vienna, and Sarah met us at a guest house we rented close to the city center. Sarah arranged all of the details of our accommodations; she even shopped and stocked our refrigerators so that we arrived to a kitchen full of snacks.

To give our team a sense of the city, Sarah arranged for one of her ministry partners to give us a walking tour of the major sites in Győr. Jerry led us all through the narrow, cobblestone streets, and he told us stories about the major churches and some of the major historical conflicts that took place in Győr over the last century. At the end of World War II in the Győr Cathedral, Bishop Apor Vilmos gave his life to protect many Hungarian women from the hands of drunk Soviet soldiers. Bishop Apor, now memorialized in one of the town's major squares, hid the women in the cathedral cellar. When the drunken Soviets broke into the cathedral cellar, intending violence against the women, the bishop intercepted them and allowed the women to escape. Unwilling to give away the women's location, the bishop enraged the Soviet soldiers, who shot and killed the priest. As we toured the cathedral, it was evident that God had worked powerfully in Győr's history.

Our schedule in Győr involved teaching classes at Sarah's school. Sarah divided my team into small groups, and each group was assigned to a classroom to serve elementary-age students in a variety of capacities. Sarah explained to our team that the students at the school came from upper middle-class families. While students did not suffer from poverty, and while everything on the outside looked healthy in this community, many of the families suffered under the ravages of alcoholism, a nationwide epidemic. "We carry the Holy Spirit with us into the classrooms," Sarah explained, "and He has the ability to break the chains of alcoholism that cover many families. Your love and care for the kids may serve to introduce them to our Lord and Savior Jesus Christ." Our team embraced this mission, and from our first day on campus I was thrilled to see a growing body of Hungarian students surrounding our team.

Bence was at the helm of this body, rallying his classmates to connect with our team. In addition to supporting our programs, Bence was excited to share all things Hungarian with us. He was generous with his cultural knowledge, and served as a wonderful guide for us at different times. When Sarah explained that our Friday activities ended with a Christmas concert in the school church, a beautiful 18th-century building in the center of the campus, Bence leaned over and whispered, "Friday is the best night of the year. The Christmas market opens up in the city and the whole place lights up with Christmas spirit!"

Although I believed Bence, I could not picture the sleepy city of Győr coming to life. Each morning as different groups of students went to work at the school, I walked with Erica and Sheffield into town where we saw an increasing number of little carts. These little carts did not look very interesting, and while cables and lights were drawn overhead, the overall feel remained calm and quiet. The many churches in town and the old Carmelite monastery were picturesque, but after just a few days, it seemed that we had seen just about everything in Győr.

One of the spots we became very familiar with was the Pink Cafe, a coffee shop that was built into the old city walls. Sarah recommended this shop to our team, and it lived up to her praise. The front of the coffee shop was painted bright pink, but the interior was eclectic and rustic. From big wooden tables, comfortable lounge chairs, and interesting fixtures spread all through the shop, the Pink Cafe was a warm, welcoming retreat and a team favorite. In between classes at the PSE, different combinations of our student team would walk across the Raba Bridge, scarves and jackets pulled tightly against the freezing wind, and warm up with big mugs of coffee and frothy lattes.

The school hosted a lively Christmas party on campus before the Christmas concert. Hundreds of families participated in the event, and there were many different booths offering homemade Hungarian delicacies. One booth sold a special family recipe of *Forralt Bor* (Hungarian mulled wine). Bence told me that certain Győr families earned great fame for their generational mulled wine recipes. The woman who sold me the cup told me the secret was in the wine: "We don't use the cheap stuff. Good mulled wine begins with a good selection of dry wine!" She waved her hand to a line of empty wine bottles, "These are all top-quality Hungarian wines." I don't want to say that the Forralt Bor changed my life, but the steaming, spicy, fruitful bouquet that floated from the mug to my face instantly became my favorite Christmas smell.

As gentle flakes of snow began to fall the evening of the Christmas concert, I stopped on the sidewalk to observe the beauty around me. Through a canopy of white lights, the snow seemed to quiet the party, and the first notes of the student ensemble floated out of the chapel. It was fun to watch and cheer for our new friends as many performed in the concert. Bence began the concert in a seat near mine, but about half way through the concert I noticed that he had joined one of the ensembles. When the final song concluded, it felt like the Christmas season had officially begun, and everyone was ready to embrace the town.

By the time we crossed the Raba Bridge, now lit up with thousands of white lights, there was a crystal glow over the entire city. The simple brown street carts were now open, strewn with garland, golden bells, bright red Poinsettia, and bursting with activity and life. Some of the carts offered custom-made holiday crafts, from hand-carved knives to wool mittens to socks and slippers. Other carts boasted giant steaming ovens, some with open flames that shot up toward hissing sausages and meats. The two most popular carts were the ones selling *Lángos* and *Kürtőskalács*. Lángos is a hot fried dough covered in a layer of sour cream, cheese, and garlic sauce. Kürtőskalács is a sweet, spiral-shaped bread baked over an open flame rotisserie style and sprinkled with sugar, cinnamon, chocolate flakes, or a combination of each.

With so many wonderful options to choose from, Erica and I made a plan to spread out our shopping and to buy small samples of different treats. We worked our way to the main square, where an open-air ice rink and giant Ferris wheel were lit up and steaming with activity. There were more people sliding across the ice rink that night than I had seen in the entire city of Győr in four days. It was clear that Bence wasn't the only one who thought this was the best night of the year in Győr.

Our final day of service at the school was bittersweet. Everyone was really excited for our next stop in Vienna, but we had all fallen in love with Sarah, Bence and the students, and the city of Győr. After teaching duties ended on our last day, Bence arranged for us to learn some traditional Hungarian dances. He and his dance teacher met us in the school cafeteria and led the team through a real dancer's training session. From running, leaping, and spinning in circles, round and round, to dropping to the floor for pushups, our college students were soon gasping for air in the hot cafeteria.

Bence smiled and laughed through the rigorous workout, and I could tell that he was genuinely surprised at the energy my team put into the dances. Bence shouted encouragement at the team, and he was once again serving us.

PART 7

FAMILY TRIPS

The following stories take place in Costa Rica and Guatemala. Neither is connected to the Around-the-World Semester program, but both are precious to my family. We traveled to Costa Rica to visit some good friends, hoping to learn from them and to support their ministry. Our trip to Guatemala was part of a university initiative started by my friend and colleague Tim Preuss.

Costa Rica: "What are Your Dreams?"

It was a simple question, but the gravity of the moment allowed me to hear it with a profound urgency: *¿Cuáles son tus sueños?*

We were in Costa Rica with my dear friends Jamie and Kathy Johnson. These two were directing a ministry in Costa Rica that focused on leadership development among at-risk youth. Their ministry was highly relational, and they were seeking to build mentor relationships with young people in the *precarios* (slums). On our first trip to visit them, we followed their team through the precario, and we played games with the kids and passed out candy. We watched them interact with the families, and we joined them as they prayed with different community members against illness, hardships, and worries. It was fun to see dozens and dozens of kids run from their homes, often tightly secured sheet metal or wooden shacks, to meet with the team members. The parents in this community clearly trusted Jamie and Kathy and their team.

Jamie's organization is called Boy with a Ball—the name capturing the most fundamental interaction between a child and a parent or mentor. The name came to Jamie one afternoon while he was tossing a ball with his infant son. "It seems that what kids want most is to be heard and to be engaged. Drug dealers and pimps have figured this out in many of the world's most desperate communities. They engage the young people and win them over to a destructive life through the promise of relationship," Jamie explained. "These criminals are very effective at youth development," Jamie often quips, "but this is not the kind of development any child wants or needs."

Jamie and his team identify themselves as a Christian ministry. They pray and share the scriptures with the young people in the precarios. They also encourage these young people to get involved in their local church communities.

The Boy with a Ball (BWAB) team also engages the young people in the slums over issues of poverty, family, and education. Jamie often talks about the different kinds of poverty: spiritual, emotional, and financial. "The most devastating of these is not financial," he warns, "but it is the spiritual and emotional poverty that really leaves these kids at greatest risk." When members of the BWAB team begin to connect with a young person, they always prioritize connecting with the young person's parents or family members. They recognize the importance of overall family health, and hope to be an encouraging source of hope for both the young people and their families. Prompted by requests from the community, the BWAB organization purchased a large property in the precario a few years into their ministry, and through it they run a tutoring center. The tutors are also part of the ministry, and they come from a very unlikely place.

During our first week in Costa Rica, we joined Jamie's lead assistant Anna on her trip to one of the local schools. The Lincoln School is an upscale private school that serves the political and business elite of Costa Rica. In addition to her role as the school basketball coach, Anna was hired to design and lead a service-learning program for Lincoln. She created a program in partnership with the BWAB tutoring center in the precario. "The kids in this program are just as much a part of our ministry focus as the kids in the precario," Anna explained as we entered the school grounds through giant iron gates and into a beautiful courtyard.

Manicured lawns wrapped neatly around fresh-painted buildings, alongside state-of-the-art sports facilities and perfect soccer fields. The sight of students in coats and ties lounging on Adirondack chairs outside classrooms made me push back on Anna's comment: "You guys consider these kids at risk?" Anna smiled. She had clearly been asked this question before, and her response brought me back to reality. She said, "In many cases, the kids from the wealthiest families have the least contact or connection with their parents. Suicide rates are often higher among the elite classes, as are the cases of substance abuse. Sadly, although these kids look good on the outside, they are often among the poorest of the poor when it comes to emotional and spiritual health." I was not prepared for this response, but as we heard stories from the students in both the Lincoln School and in the precario, what Anna said began to make sense. I was irrationally connecting affluence with health.

The students in Anna's service-learning class were prepping for their Thursday afternoon tutoring session in the precario. They had collected school supplies from Lincoln students and families, and they were excited to interact with the precario kids. Many of the Lincoln students had been deeply impacted by the tutoring ministry, and although few were Christians, they all recognized something sacred about the work they were doing. One young lady stood in front of the class and shared a story about one of the little girls she had worked with the prior week. She described how poor the little girl was, holes in her tiny shoes, stained blouse, torn skirt, but how amazing it was to see her working hard and maintaining a hopeful attitude. "She was so joyful, too," the young lady explained. Several of the other students in the room nodded and expressed agreement by sharing similar stories. She went on, "The kids and the families in the precario are just like us. They want to be loved, they want to laugh with friends, they want to have fun and succeed. We have so much stuff, more than we need, it feels so good to share with them."

When we left the Lincoln School I was silent. I had completely misjudged the rich kids, assuming they were all very content and safe. I also assumed that they would misjudge the precario kids and look down on them. Instead, through Anna and the BWAB team's coaching, the Lincoln students had very clear vision, and they were being changed by what they were now able to recognize. My eyes were also changing, but the greatest vision correction would not take place until Friday at 1:00am.

We teamed up with the Lincoln students in the precario Thursday afternoon. I coached a little boy through a reading packet, and then we colored in a few pages together. Across the table from me was Noah, a 16-year-old junior from the Lincoln School. Noah wore a pressed blue Polo shirt and designer jeans. His hair was trimmed and he looked like a professional. He was helping a little boy with some math problems, but he was also managing to interact with a little boy who was pushing a truck on the floor by his feet. Noah was working through math problems one minute, and then dropped to the floor the next minute to play with the little truck boy. Whenever I got stumped with a Spanish word, I would tap Noah's arm and he would smile and translate for me. This Lincoln School student was more than a preppy rich kid; he was fully engaged with the work at hand and his attitude inspired me.

After the tutoring session, Jamie and Anna asked us if we would join them on some house visits. "It would be great to have a few of you students join us for translation help, if you have time," Anna said to the group of Lincoln kids. Noah and a few others stepped up, and we all followed Jamie and Anna. After several winding turns, ducking under active electrical wires and other low-hanging structures, we entered a darker section of the precario where the sewage ran a little thicker in between the wood and metal homes. Jamie knocked on a door and motioned for Noah and me to follow him inside. We stepped down into a living room and were met by two women and an 18-year-old boy. The young man, Jose, had an apple-sized lump on the side of his skull, and it was apparent that he had some pretty serious disabilities. The women in the room, Jose's mother and grandmother, asked Jamie to pray for Jose's healing. Before Jamie started Jose motioned for me to join him on the couch. His grandmother jumped up and offered me her spot. I wanted to insist that she stay, but I could tell they wanted to honor me and I did not want to offend them.

When I sat down Jose put his arm around my shoulders and smiled. He patted my shoulder, pulled lightly at the edge of my blonde hair, and said "Este hombre es un Vikingo." The entire household erupted in laughter, including Noah and Jamie. Noah leaned down and said, "He thinks you look like a Viking." I laughed and flexed my arms; Jose clapped and smiled. After joking around a bit more, Jose suddenly grabbed my hand and placed it on his head. He said, "Quiero que el Vikingo rece por mí." Noah leaned down again, "He wants you to pray for him...uh, he said he wants the Viking to pray for him." I smiled and nodded. When I asked Noah to translate the prayer, I could tell he was uncomfortable. He looked at Jamie, but Jamie just nodded, stepped forward, and put his hand on Jose's shoulder. With this encouragement, Noah leaned in and put his hand on Jose's shoulder. He said, "Ready when you are, Mr. Viking."

As I prayed for God's healing touch, for the grace and love of Jesus Christ to fill the home, and for faith to strengthen Jose for a challenging journey, Noah kept pace with me. He matched my tone, and at the end of the prayer, when I felt my eyes fill up with tears, I could tell that Noah was getting choked up too. We were all moved by Jose's kindness and joy. He had a sweet smile and a really engaging warmth about him. As I finished my prayer and took my hand away from the tumor on his head, I really hoped to see the bulge in his skull disappear. "Please Jesus, just like in the New Testament when you healed so many sick and dying men and women, heal Jose," I prayed in my spirit.

When it was time to leave, Jose motioned for me to help him stand. I gave him a big hug and squeezed his shoulder: "Mi hermano." He grabbed my shoulder in response and said, "Mi hermano Vikingo!" As we walked back to the tutoring center, I asked Noah if he'd ever translated a prayer. He said, "No, but I really loved that. I really thought that we were going to see that bump disappear. I've never heard people talk to God like that." Jamie told me later that moments like these were the best parts of mentoring. He said, "You can preach to young people, give them books to read, or even pray over them yourself, but in the end they have to see you walking out what you believe."

I don't know why God chooses to heal at times and not at other times, but I continue to pray. I pray for people I love, and people I care about. I pray trusting, knowing that God loves every woman, every man, and every child. Noah saw us enter into a real conversation with God, and it changed his life. Even though nothing miraculous happened at the material level, it was clear to all of us that God was present in Jose's living room that afternoon.

By 11:30pm on Friday night we filled two large thermoses with coffee and stuffed several packs of cookies into a few backpacks. Before departure we circled up in Jamie and Kathy's living room to pray. Jamie, Kathy, and the BWAB team members prayed for different ladies by name—young girls who were stuck in prostitution and trying to get out. Although I was not worried about any particular danger, I was nervous about this trip downtown. I had a feeling something powerful and unexpected was going to happen, and I hoped that I would be ready.

We parked in an area where there was a large concentration of bars and restaurants. Music poured out from several different directions, all blending in a festive, chaotic way in the streets. The sidewalk space in front of the bars was jammed with people, mostly Americans and Europeans, and we sidestepped some drunken chaos as Jamie led us to the end of the street. Jamie pointed to a blue building near the middle of the city square and leaned toward me: "That hotel is infamous for child prostitution. The government and the police allow it to continue in business, because the owners make such generous political donations." He explained that the hotel's primary clientele is made up of American businessmen. I felt a wave of nausea and anger sweep over me. I wanted to run into the building, to rescue the children, and to burn the place to the ground. The evil that stood guard at the entrance of that hotel was bold and vicious. It drew support from principalities and powers, government agencies and a powerful police force. It was a terrible feeling to know that children were being tortured in that building, and that we could do nothing to stop it.

Jamie pointed across the street to a poorly lit parking lot and a group of young ladies. "I think I see Veronica over there," he said with a smile. We crossed the street and Jamie shouted a greeting to the young ladies. Our team spread out, and we began cracking open cookie packets and pouring coffee. The ladies were kind to us, but at many levels I knew they were trapped behind just as much barbed wire and muscle as the children in the blue hotel. My vision changed when Jamie led me up to Veronica. He spoke in rapid Spanish, but I knew he said something like, "Veronica, I want to introduce you to my friend John. He is a Viking." Veronica laughed and reached to shake my hand with a smile. Veronica was a beautiful girl, probably in her mid-twenties. She was full of energy, and as she called out to various girls in the group, it was clear that she was one of the leaders. Two or three girls stood close to her, almost tucking themselves into her wake.

Veronica leaned forward and whispered something to Jamie. When he smiled and nodded, Veronica turned and led us through the group into a darker section of the parking lot. As the group parted my eyes fell on a 12-year-old girl standing by herself with her arms folded across her chest. As we approached her, she looked at the ground and slid her right foot from side to side. "Isabelle!" shouted Veronica with her trademark energy, "Estos son mis amigos" (These are my friends) " y uno de ellos es un vikingo" (and one of them is a Viking) Isabella smiled and hugged Veronica. She shook our hands and smiled. Jamie and Anna jumped right into a conversation with Isabella, and the pace of their speech was too much for me. I just stood there holding the coffee thermos, watching Jamie and Anna, and praying that Jesus would perform a miracle for this little girl.

I don't know if Jamie suddenly decided to speak slowly for my benefit, or if the Lord just gave me some linguistic grace, but I heard "¿Cuáles son tus sueños?" (What are your dreams?) The question sent a chill down my arms, and I had to put the coffee thermos down. Isabella's eyes filled with tears, and she began to describe her love for cooking. She dreamed of going to culinary school and becoming a chef in a restaurant. Jamie and Anna stepped closer to her, both were excited by Isabella's answer. Anna put her hand on Isabella's shoulder and said, "Podemos ayudarle" (We can help you). They described a friend they had who owned a cafe in town. They also told Isabella that they could help her get into classes at the local culinary school. Isabella pressed her hands together, lifted them to her chin, and squealed with sweet joy. Jamie told her that if she met them at the BWAB office in the morning, they could get her an interview and she could start work right away; she could also start taking classes right away. Isabella nodded and smiled. Anna gave her the address, and told her what to wear.

Veronica came back over when she heard Isabella squeal. She handed Isabella a small ring of keys and told her to go home for a good night of rest.

As we drove back to Jamie and Kathy's house later that night, I kept hearing Jamie's question in my head, "¿Cuáles son tus sueños?" I think these were the most beautiful words I'd ever heard. There was an unexpected power in this phrase that cut through a wall of barbed wire. I saw a fortress fall that night, and witnessed the release of a real-life princess.

Guatemala:
"Hurry Up,
Wait, and Listen"

From the roof of the Candelaria Hotel in Antigua, I could see the intermittent eruptions of a giant volcano: Volcan de Fuego. This beautiful volcano is one of the centerpieces of the Antigua skyline, standing over twelve thousand feet above the city. On our final day in Guatemala, I rose early to sit on our rooftop terrace. A giant gray cloud burst through the cone of Volcan de Fuego as I took a seat on a patio chair. This was my fourth trip to Guatemala in two years as a guide, representative, and consultant for Concordia University's Guatemala Initiative. Another gray cloud rose above Volcan de Fuego, and I thought about the many frustrations that I'd walked through during my time in Guatemala. Like the force of energy that is required to build behind each of Fuego's eruptions, pressure must mount in a person's spirit before he or she is ready to change and grow in significant ways.

We launched the Guatemala Initiative with a faculty-student trip in the spring of 2015. The vision was to form a mutually beneficial partnership with a small village called El Progreso. On that first trip, we met with a group of community leaders called the COCODE. Our goal was to find different ways in which the university could support the village. One of the issues that the COCODE revealed to our team on the first visit was that hundreds of the villagers struggled with chronic diarrhea. The COCODE was not united behind a single cause, but many expressed concerns about water quality.

After our return to campus the director of the university initiative, Tim Preuss, asked me to lead the next trip. Solving the water quality issue was my top concern, and I put together a team to brainstorm ways of approaching the problem. Our research led us to make contact with a surf company in Southern California that had had some success with water purification initiatives in other Latin American countries. When we reached out to Hurley they connected us with an organization called "Waves for Water." This nonprofit sent us piles of materials about a top-quality product they developed for use in poor mountain villages. Each of their filters was built to purify one million gallons of water each; the system worked with a simple hand pump and a five-gallon bucket.

I contacted our missionary host in Guatemala about how best to introduce the filters, and he suggested that we bring ten filters for a trial among the COCODE in November. I co-led the November trip with our campus pastor Jonathan Ruehs, who helped organize and design a four-day Bible camp for the children in the village. My wife Erica and our three children were also part of the November 2015 team, along with several Concordia students. Our team had three purposes: leading a Bible camp, writing biographies about the village leaders, and piloting the water filtration system.

I knew we had a problem when we met with the COCODE that November and only three of the leaders were interested in trying out the filter. The message, though loud and clear, did not compute in my mind, and I pressed forward with what I discerned to be the best course of action for the village. We discovered on the November trip that many infants died each year from dehydration and malnutrition. These clues, as well as the water report that we collected, proved to me that water quality was the key to improved health in the village. Adding to my research, I followed one of the village leaders on a six-mile hike, starting at the source of the water line, winding through fields and farms, and ending at a small concrete water tank above El Progreso. The water line was cracked in several places along the route. These cracks, as explained by our missionary host, allowed insecticides, animal feces, and countless other contaminants to enter the water source.

At the end of the line we arrived at the water-holding tank, and the community leader began to explain his vision for improved health in the village. An additional water tank, he explained, would allow the village to have a more readily accessible water supply. At this time, due to the fact that the village was growing and expanding, the village exhausted its water supply at about noon each day. These concerns seemed valid to me, but I was more determined to stop the flow of contaminated water into each home. I was ready with a water-filter supplier, and I had some friends back home who were ready to write checks to see this project completed. Unfortunately, I was unable to hear the concerns voiced by the community leader.

When we returned to the United States, I began fundraising with the goal of putting a water filter in all 200 homes in El Progreso. We raised the money with the help of a $5,000 matching grant from the Keith Family Foundation, and the goal was reached within just a few months. The next trip was slated for May of 2016, and due to some last-minute complications, the team leader had to back out at the last minute. I was more than willing to take the helm of another team. To make matters even sweeter, this team included nine nurses from the Concordia nursing school. The nurses were prepared to perform a well-visit examination for each of the men and women in the community. This project would be a great compliment to the water-quality education I hoped to lead in the village. My water class would culminate with the gifting of water filters for each village family.

When we arrived in Guatemala that May, the trip felt more like a family reunion than a mission trip. We had a great fondness for our guesthouse, the Peregrino Inn, which was located in a small city called La Union. The owner of the inn roasted his own coffee beans on the property, and the fragrance of the roasting was delightful. Also in La Union, we developed a love for a diner called Fabi's Place. Fabi's was owned and operated by Fabi and her mother Sandra. They always allowed us to reserve their covered patio, and served us traditional Guatemalan breakfasts and dinners. Fabi and Sandra also packed lunches-to-go for us to take up to the village. The homemade care they invested in these meals resulted in some wonderful and very memorable dining experiences. During our meals at Fabi's Place, the owner and head chef Sandra would always visit with us. I think her primary desire was to hug and tickle my four-year-old son Sheffield, but she was always friendly to our teams too.

The drive from La Union up to El Progreso took approximately 30 minutes, and it involved an incredible tour through coffee plantations and a thick green forest. While riding in the truck bed looked like fun to Sheffield, after a few minutes in the bed he always migrated to the interior cab with me. The bumpy dirt road put him to sleep every morning and every afternoon, and given the number of miles he would run while playing with the children in the village, Erica and I soon recognized the importance of these power naps.

On our first trip to El Progreso that fall, Sheffield developed two very good friends: Jacqueline and Jimmy. His mission, on arrival in the village, was to find these two buddies. It was fun to watch his big brown eyes scan the groups of children when our truck entered the village. Jimmy and Jacqueline were always part of the greeting party, and we let Sheffield scamper off with these two while we greeted the village leadership. These men and women were dear to our hearts, and I was really excited to bring them such a fantastic team of nurses. On our November trip to El Progreso, the COCODE mentioned that very few of the villagers knew much about basic hygiene and that they would benefit from some health education. The nursing team had prepared several classes in this area, and as mentioned, they planned to offer a free health review or *well visit* for any interested villagers.

The tradition in the village was for the COCODE to circle up with our team in the community center shortly after our arrival. During these meetings they voiced their appreciation for our continued support. They also insisted that we share names during these meetings, and that we continue to build friendships. I was really excited to start the well visit and the water-filtration program, but I knew better than to rush this part of the process. If only I had allowed my respect for this relational process to inform the rest of my thinking and planning for the village.

After the COCODE meeting, several of the leaders left to gather the villagers for their well visits. The COCODE had made a schedule for each family in the village, knowing that many needed medical attention. The line soon began to grow outside the community center, and our team went to work. Jack and Naomi were recruited by the nursing team to help write down medical information, measure each patient's height and weight, as well as conduct vision tests. From our arrival in the village each morning at 9:00am until our departure at 3:00pm, Sheffield ran from one end of the village to the other. He played games, built dirt forts, and wrangled with all sorts of farm animals with a fun posse of kids his age. It was always fun to listen to his conversations with the village kids, none of whom spoke a word of English. They chatted all day long, laughed and designed projects together, but the language barrier never slowed down the fun.

At the end of the week my failure to really listen and understand the desires of the community and its leadership bore fruit in a very frustrating event. With 200 water filters ready for distribution, only 37 families arrived to attend the water education class I had designed. It became painfully clear that the village had no vision for water filtration, and among the 37 people who ended up coming to get a filter, I believe only a few really understood the necessity. Most of the families who showed up to my class did so because they loved me and cared for me. These were friends, but they did not share my vision, and thus my project was a total failure.

The COCODE leaders apologized for the poor turnout, but that moment of failure gave me some instant clarity. As frustrating as it was to fail, I did not want to waste any more time with my own planning. My ears were open, at last, and I wanted to hear more about the water tank idea. This project had been mentioned by a few more of the COCODE at the beginning of the week, but in my laser-like focus on filters, I did not listen. Now, with over $8,000 of unwanted water filters stacked in boxes against the wall of the community center, I was very alert.

I followed the COCODE leaders up to the site of the current water tank. It was a steep climb through the forest, and I tried to imagine hauling bags of cement and rebar up this path. We would need a team of 300 if we hoped to pull this off in a seven-day visit. With each step up the muddy path the doubts started to grow in my spirit. Sixto, Josue, and Eduardo explained that the current tank had been built by the government many years prior when El Progreso had only 75 families. Having more than doubled in the last ten years, the village drained this tank by noon each day—meaning that no one in the village had access to water during the afternoon and evening hours. An additional tank would provide water for the families of El Progreso, but if designed as they hoped, it could also help the village adjacent to theirs. Now that I was listening, I recognized that the COCODE had concerns far greater than their own village. They were thinking about friends and families farther down the mountain who were struggling against greater limitations than the people of El Progreso. I was deeply moved by the purposes I now recognized in the COCODE leadership.

My regret in running blindly forward with the filters was significant, but I knew that this was no time to sulk. At our final meeting I told the COCODE that I would help them raise money for the new tank. A few of them, usually quite reserved, jumped out of their seats, clapped, and hugged me. We'd made a course correction, and I was determined to get it right this time.

When I returned to California, I met with Tim Preuss. I shared my regrets about misfiring with the filters, but he was very encouraging. He helped me put together a fundraising team, and by the next week we had secured significant gifts from both the Keith Family Foundation and the Michael Chang Family Foundation. By late summer, with the addition of more than 100 small, individual donations, we raised the $17,000 needed to construct the new water tank. We sent the funds, and we received word from our missionary host that the COCODE would begin the project immediately.

I was very excited to be asked to lead the November team, and delighted to share the leadership with one of our Concordia theology faculty members and his wife, Scott and Julie Steigemeyer. This wonderful couple helped us design a Bible camp for the El Progreso children as well as a series of sewing classes for the village women. The sewing class was born out of a request for business development from the COCODE. They knew of several women in the community who could not work in the coffee fields, nor could they travel into La Union for work. Many women wanted to learn to sew, and they were motivated to start small businesses in El Progreso. Scott and Julie were fantastic teammates for Erica and me. Their creativity and energy were huge blessings as we trained our small team for the November trip.

All through the fall semester I received word that the COCODE were making headway on the water tank. We would not need to bring students for the construction project, as more than 75 men from the village were dedicating hours each day to the construction of the tank. This news came at a time when our student team was not only very small, but the members were mostly interested in helping with the sewing classes and the Bible camp. Another boost to the team came when two wonderful youth leaders from Bethany Lutheran Church expressed interest in joining the team. The Steigemeyers, Erica, and I connected with Kayleigh and Andy right away, and we could tell that these two would add some serious leadership strength to the team.

We entered the village to the same kind of fanfare as the last two trips. Kids surrounded our truck, Sheffield recognized his friends, and he was off. The rest of us gathered in the community center with the COCODE, but there was something different about this meeting. Smiles were bigger, and while the COCODE were committed to circling up and sharing names and building relationships, I could tell that there was something brewing beneath the surface. We shared our plans for the Bible camp and the sewing classes, and the COCODE expressed visible gratitude.

At the end of our meeting Sixto, Josue, and Eduardo led Jack, Scott, and me up to the new water tank. A team of 50 men were working in different spots, all around the tank. The foundation of the tank, as well as one side of the tank were complete. A wooden scaffolding surrounded the tank, and I was told that the men would finish the sides and then the top of the tank in the next few days. Sixto asked the men to gather up for a few words. He introduced Jack, Scott, and me and the men broke out in applause. A few stepped forward to pat our shoulders; it was clear that Sixto had mentioned that we were the friends who provided the funds for the tank. I greeted the men and expressed my gratitude for the friendship we'd developed with the people of El Progreso. I told the men how happy it made me that my children and my wife Erica and I were loved so kindly and affectionately by the people of El Progreso. I mentioned also how impressive it was to see so much of the water tank completed in such a short time. I introduced Scott, and I told them that he would be saying a blessing over the water tank. What I did not expect was to be moved to tears by Scott's blessing. His words and his prayer, spoken boldly and confidently over the tank and over the men gathered there, really touched my heart. When we lifted our heads at the end of the prayer, I saw several of the big, tough Guatemalan men wipe tears from their eyes, too.

The Bible camp and the sewing classes were packed that week with energetic participants. Julie used some of the time during the sewing class to share about her faith in Christ, and the women were very receptive. Naomi stuck close

GUATEMALA: "HURRY UP, WAIT, AND LISTEN"

to Julie and loved interacting with the women and creating interesting crafts. Erica, as always, bonded with many of the mothers of the children Sheffield played with. Erica was often invited into homes where she prayed for different families—her laughter and kindness seemed to open doors for our team all over the village. Andy and Kayleigh attracted mobs of children around the community center and down to the village soccer field, where they led an entire week of games and events.

As I sat on the rooftop of the Candelaria Hotel in Antigua that morning, I watched Volcan de Fuego erupt over and over again. I thought about my journey with the COCODE in El Progreso and all that we had accomplished together. It was the pressure of disappointment and the pressure from goals unmet that had to mount in my spirit before I was willing and able to hear the leaders in El Progreso. When the layers of my own stubbornness were blown away, my ears and then my heart were opened to real friendship. In this place of humble clarity, I was able to truly partner with friends and to make a difference.

FINAL NOTES

When I started taking short term mission trips in my early teens, I thought of myself as a missionary. After over forty years of these kinds of missional experiences, however, my view has changed. The missionary is the faithful servant on the ground, in country, and on assignment in a particular community. As a visitor to any given mission project, I no longer consider myself a missionary but a servant, a student, and a friend. As we lead ATW teams, we emphasize this perspective. Students return from our trips with new ideas, increased levels of understanding, and broader vision about God's faithfulness to His children all around the world.

When we complete an ATW trip, we encourage the student travelers to continue their support of the missionaries and churches we visited. Whether it be through prayer, finances, or storytelling, our support for the church worldwide must continue when we return home.

If one or more of the stories in this book touched you in a particularly significant way, and you would like to make a financial contribution, please reach out to our team at Bose Road Ministries (www.boseroad.org). Bose Road is a nonprofit ministry we started to help Concordia University Irvine run the ATW Semester program. Bose Road also helps churches and schools set up high-impact educational and missional experiences. At the Bose Road website you will find more travel stories, as well as additional ways to follow our journey.

SPECIAL THANKS

The Around-the-World Semester was made possible by God's grace and the generous hearts and minds of many wonderful people. The danger of a section like this is that someone is always left off. As I remember more people to thank, I will be posting about them on our website, www.boseroad.org.

In alphabetical order:

Concordia University Irvine: Over the last nineteen years, Concordia University Irvine has become a family to me, to Erica, and to our three children. We are so thankful for this Christ-loving, generous community. The upper administration provided many green lights for Adam and I as we developed the ATW program. Support came from President Kurt Krueger and Provost Mary Scott in the early years, and most recently President Michael Thomas and Provost Scott Ashmon. Your courage as leaders has allowed us to freely develop a very special program with many moving parts. Deans Terry Olson and Bret Taylor continue to offer kind and generous support before and after the trips. Each of these men has helped me navigate some challenging circumstances with wisdom.

Kevin Davenport: My pastor and mentor for over twenty years, Kevin is a faithful supporter of our ATW program. He and the Saddleback Covenant Church community have not only given our program generous financial support, but they have prayed for us faithfully, they have stayed connected with us as we've traveled, and upon reentry, they have offered us opportunities to share